60 YEARS

OF INTEGRATION

Building Upon The Legacy

THE UNIVERSITY OF MISSISSIPPI

If there is anywhere in the world that can solve the problem of our time it's Mississippi. My goal is to move Mississippi from the bottom to the top, and we ain't there yet.

–James Meredith

JAMES MEREDITH

Breaking the Barrier

Celebrating the 60th Anniversary of James Meredith's
Enrollment at the University of Mississippi

Edited by
Kathleen W. Wickham

Yoknapatawpha Press
Oxford, Mississippi

Published by Yoknapatawpha Press, P.O. Box 248, Oxford,
Mississippi 38655

The publisher gratefully acknowledges permissions
from the following publishers to reprint excerpts:

Doyle, William, *An American Insurrection: James Meredith and the Battle of Oxford, Mississippi, 1962* (Anchor Books/Random House, 2001).

Gallagher, Henry, *James Meredith and the Ole Miss Riot: A Soldier's Story* (University Press of Mississippi, 2012).

Gilliam, Dorothy, *Trailblazer: A Pioneering Journalist's Fight to Make the Media Look More Like America* (Center Point Books/Hachette, 2019).

Meredith, James, *Three Years in Mississippi* (Bloomington, IN: Indiana University Press, 1966).

Wickham, Kathleen, *We Believed We Were Immortal: Twelve Reporters Who Covered the 1962 Integration Crisis at Ole Miss* (Yoknapatawpha Press, 2017).

Wilkie, Curtis, *Dixie: A Personal Odyssey Through Events That Shaped the Modern South* (Lisa Drew Books/Scribner, 2001).

Winter, William F., Afterword, *Riot: Witness to Anger and Change*, by Edwin E. Meek (Yoknapatawpha Press, 2015).

ISBN 978-0-916242-90-9

Book and cover design by Chad Murchison.

Cover photo by Bill Miles, used with permission from the Department of Archives and Special Collections, University of Mississippi.

CONTENTS

FOREWORD
By Jesse Holland

Jesse Holland
(Photo by Doug Sanford)

If you encountered James Meredith walking around the Grove or strolling through the Lyceum, you probably wouldn't notice him. I know I didn't.

It was at an University of Mississippi event in the 1990s when we first met. I knew who he was of course: My parents—public school teachers—made sure to educate me on African American history in Mississippi and around the United States above and beyond the curriculum required by the public schools.

So, I already knew the legend of James Meredith, the brave man who defied the white racists including Mississippi's governor to attend the flagship university of the Magnolia State, smashing down barriers for African Americans including my mother, who in the 1970s received her master's degree from the university.

The few photos that I'd seen from that time showed a proud Black man, nattily dressed in a suit and tie, pocket square firmly in place, standing tall with a serious expression on his face, striding purposefully between his escorts, defiant in the face of screaming, rabid white supremacists. To me, he strode like a giant, above the racist and bigoted concerns of the mob, head above the crowd, seemingly existing on another plane where men demand respect, ignore ignorance, and strive to improve themselves no matter what

1

obstacles life and American institutional racism place in their way.

I was expecting a physical colossus: The great and powerful James Meredith, slayer of racism, the conqueror of Ole Miss, the herald of a Black Mississippi to come, the progenitor of future University of Mississippi students like me. A man's man who stood up to racist politicians, bloodthirsty mobs, prejudiced professors and students and an indifferent world who refused to join him in fighting injustices perpetrated by the white power structure.

What I didn't expect was the real James Meredith: a gray-bearded, quiet, humble Black man wearing a hat who looked like he was not trying to draw attention to himself. This diminutive man was quick to smile, but as he slowly walked through the crowd, Meredith often looked like he'd prefer for all of us to leave him alone with his memories.

I stepped forward, parted the crowd, and thrust my hand out for him to shake. Meredith, who had been laughingly acknowledging someone else in the crowd, looked up into my eyes as he grasped my hand with a strong grip.

And when we locked eyes was when I met the real James Meredith. Looking into his eyes, I saw the man I expected: steely, determined, courageous, unyielding. Flustered, I remember mumbling something along the lines of a "Thank you," or some such. James Meredith nodded and kept walking through the crowd, shaking hands and nodding to people he knew and people who just wanted to be in his presence.

To this day, I remember his profound scrutiny, the history he carried in every step, the weight he still carries for his home state and his alma mater and the debt we still owe him.

He was not what I expected. He was more.

But that is the story of James Meredith: a refusal to compromise, a man who does what he thinks is right regardless of expectation or cost, a maverick who wrote his own story and his own legend. Meredith could have been a John Lewis, a Marion Berry, a Jesse Jackson, a civil rights icon who led people nationally and internationally and preached freedom and equality from coast to coast.

Instead, he walked his own path, forever changing the road

for the people who came behind him in Mississippi and the deep South.

For many, James Meredith is a giant, a man who walked alone when necessary to achieve his goals yet was not afraid to confront the crowds of injustice, resistance, and racism. He is a man who could have made anything of himself, and yet sacrificed his name, his body and his life to become a symbol of resistance to racism at Ole Miss, in Mississippi and the South.

Unknown to many outside of grainy black and white photographs and video, Meredith to this day holds a unique place in Mississippi history, Ole Miss history and African American history.

But for many, there are only two images of James Meredith, Meredith being escorted into the University of Mississippi by federal marshals and Meredith writhing on a Mississippi road after being shot by a white terrorist during a freedom march.

A man's life, summed up by two images of violence and hatred.

Instead of a man, many people see a symbol of resistance, a symbol of justice. That's how we want to remember him, like the James Meredith Memorial on the university campus. The James Meredith frozen in time, striding forward through the crowd stepping into an unknown future of equal opportunity and justice for all.

That's why many of us are so surprised at first in his presence: He's real? A flesh and blood man with thoughts, opinions, and beliefs of his own outside of racism, Ole Miss and the 1960s? This is also why many were shocked to find out that Meredith in his later life eschewed commonly assumed African American politics by supporting two of the most divisive and racist American politicians: North Carolina Sen. Jesse Helms, an avid opponent to civil rights legislation, and endorsing for Louisiana governor former Klansman David Duke.

We wanted a symbol, an icon, a representation of all of us. We got James Meredith, a man who had the courage to go his own way against all expectations, refused to kowtow to common expectations of himself and what he should be and didn't care what the world thought about his person, his politics, or his goals.

His determination to be himself and not what anyone else expected him to be is likely why James Meredith will always be a Mississippi hero and solely a national footnote and not a civil rights giant like Martin Luther King, Jesse Jackson, Shirley Chisholm, Malcolm X, John Lewis, Fannie Lou Hamer and others.

His is not a name that will be celebrated everywhere, though it should be. His impact was more local and personal to the University of Mississippi and to the state of Mississippi, but no one can envision an Ole Miss today without his courageous efforts.

Since James Meredith, thousands of African American students have attended Ole Miss, including my parents, my siblings and myself. There have been Black Ole Miss athletes, scholars, journalists, and students who all owe our start to the courageous stand Meredith made. Without him, the University of Mississippi we know today would not exist.

James Meredith may not be a physical giant, but he will forever loom large on the campus of the University of Mississippi and in the South. And that is as it should be.

Jesse Holland is an American journalist, author, television personality and educator. He grew up in Orange Mound near Memphis, the nation's first African-American neighborhood. He was the second African-American editor of the *Daily Mississippian*, the student newspaper of the University of Mississippi. Holland was a distinguished visiting professor of ethics in journalism at the University of Arkansas, and served as guest host on C-SPAN's Washington Journal. His books include *"Black Men Built the Capital: Discovering African-American History In and Around Washington, DC,"* and *"The Invisibles: The Untold Story of African-American Slaves in the White House,"* which was awarded a silver medal in U.S. history from the Independent Publishers Association.

Insurrection

by James Meredith

From *Three Years in Mississippi,*
Indiana University Press, 1966

James Meredith registering for classes, Oct. 1, 1962
*(Photo by Ed Meek courtesy Department of Archives and Special Collections,
University of Mississippi)*

September 30 and October 1, 1962, may well go down in history as one of the supreme tests of the United States. Insurrection against the United States by the state of Mississippi became on these two days a reality.

The state of Mississippi had clearly shown its intention not only to threaten to use violence, but to use it. In the face of this direct challenge the federal government had no choice but to act to enforce its authority. President John F. Kennedy acted at the crucial moment on September 30, 1962, by issuing a proclamation and executive order which concluded:

". . . I hereby authorize the Secretary of Defense to call into the active military service of the United States, as he may deem appropriate to carry out the purposes of this order, any or all of the units of the Army National Guard and of the Air National Guard of the State of Mississippi to serve in the active military service of the United States for an indefinite period and until relieved by appropriate orders."

U.S. Marshals land at Oxford/University Airport, Sept. 30, 1962
(Photo by Ed Meek courtesy Department of Archives and Special Collections, University of Mississippi)

The call went out all over the United States for U.S. marshals, border patrolmen, and federal prison guards to report for duty. As political appointees in their local areas the marshals were not fighting men, nor were all of them trained in the art of riot or mob control. The usual background for a marshal is some form of police work. Moreover, due to the unusual nature of this assignment, it was necessary for the chiefs to have training sessions at Millington Naval Air Station for the marshals.

In the meantime, the Army arrived in great force. The entire Naval Air Station had been turned into a drill field. One of the most notable things to me was that Negro officers and men were with the army units. Many of the drill sergeants were Negro noncommissioned officers.

After my last futile attempt to enroll it became evident that I was becoming more and more isolated. There were no more advisers at this point. Of course, I could understand the position of the NAACP Legal Defense and Educational Fund. Since the case was beyond the legal field and they were so far removed from the scene it would have been unwise for them to advise me. Finally, on September 29 I was left on my own.

Gov. Ross Barnett (center) arrives at the
University of Mississippi campus, 1962
*(Photo by Ed Meek courtesy Department of Archives and Special Collections,
University of Mississippi)*

My greatest uncertainty was the speculation about a deal between the federal government and Ross Barnett, governor of the state of Mississippi. It must always be remembered that I was a Negro in Mississippi, and I was acutely aware of my history as a Negro. The question that we now faced—the extension of citizenship rights to the Negro—was not new. Certainly, in the past, deals had been made between the federal government and Mississippi. How could I, a Negro, who had never once received my due, and who knew of no single occasion where my forebears on the Negro side had received his due, not be concerned about the prospect of deal-making, especially when no official of the federal government would commit himself or his government as to the exact extent of its involvement?

"I speak to you now in the moment of the greatest crisis since the War Between the States. We must either submit to the unlawful dictates of the federal government or stand up like men and tell them, and say to them plainly, 'Never.'" –Governor Ross Barnett

(Photo by Ed Meek courtesy Department of Archives and Special Collections, University of Mississippi)

September 30th was a Sunday. The previous day Barnett had experienced his greatest triumph when he was cheered at the "Ole Miss" football game in Jackson. General Edwin Walker had issued his famous call for volunteers to come to Mississippi. Activity was at a peak at Millington. We would go today.

Late in the afternoon we boarded the "Ole Miss" special. Ironically, it was the first time we changed planes. The Florida pilot had returned home. We had a new plane and a new pilot, but my traveling companions—Chief Marshal John McShane and justice department attorney John Doar—were still with me. We flew to Oxford and had to circle the airport for some time before receiving clearance to land.

U.S. Deputy Marshals arrive in Oxford
(Photo by Ed Meek courtesy Department of Archives and Special Collections, University of Mississippi)

The Oxford airport was unrecognizable. There were rows of Air Force and transport planes and hundreds of marshals. The two most noticeable things were the floodlights and the tense atmosphere. We got off the plane and passed through a host of men wearing U.S. deputy marshal armbands, all of whom seemed to close in on us. We slowly proceeded in a caravan to Baxter Hall, arriving between dusk and darkness. The campus was completely deserted. There were no obvious signs that school was in session. The entire student body had either caught the "Barnett Special" train to Jackson or found their own means of getting to the football game. Without ceremony we moved into Baxter Hall to spend the first night. There was no dorm chief present to give me the rules of the hall.

I suppose one could call my quarters an apartment. Since they knew some government men would be staying with me, I had been assigned two bedrooms, a living room, and a bathroom. The first thing that I did was make my bed. When the trouble started, I could not see or hear very much of it. Most of the events occurred at the other end of the campus. I did not look out the window. I think I read a newspaper and went to bed around ten o'clock. I was awakened several times in the night by noise and shooting, but it was not near the hall. I had no way of knowing what was going on. Some of the students in my dormitory banged on their doors or threw bottles in the hallways, but I slept pretty well.

Student protestors gather at the Lyceum where
U.S. Marshals are positioned.
*(Photo by Ed Meek courtesy Department of Archives and Special Collections,
University of Mississippi)*

I woke up about 6:30 in the morning and looked out and saw the troops. There was a slight smell of tear gas in my room. I still did not know what had gone on during the night. I did not find out, until some marshals came and told me that many people had been hurt and two were killed.

Later some newspapermen asked if I thought attending the university was worth all the death and destruction. Of course, I was sorry! I hadn't wanted this to happen. I believe it could have been prevented by responsible political leadership in Mississippi. As for the federal government, the President and the Attorney General had all the intelligence facilities at their disposal. I believe that they handled it to the best of their ability. It could have been much worse if they had waited any longer. Social change is a painful thing, but the method by which it is achieved depends upon the people at the top. Here they were totally opposed—the state against the federal government. There was bound to be trouble, and there was.

Ole Miss students protest Meredith's admission.
(Photo by Ed Meek courtesy Department of Archives and Special Collections, University of Mississippi)

There was no lingering or turning back now. At eight o'clock the three of us—McShane, Doar, and Meredith—with a retinue of marshals and soldiers left Baxter Hall. The signs of strife and warfare from the night before were everywhere. But at this moment the power of the United States was supreme. Even the Mississippi National Guard had proven that its first loyalty was to the Commander-in-Chief of the Armed Forces of the United States, the President.

James Meredith accompanied by Chief Marshal James McShane and federal attorney John Does heads to class.
(Photo by Ed Meek courtesy Department of Archives and Special Collections, University of Mississippi)

11

The border patrol car in which we rode to the administration building was a shattered example of the violence of social change. When we used this car in our first attempt to enroll on September 20, 1962, the sedan was spotless. Now it was battered and smashed. Bullet holes riddled the sides. The windows were all shot out. McShane sent one of the deputies back into Baxter Hall to get a couple of Army blankets to put over the back seat so that we could sit down. The marshals had suffered as well. It would have been hard to find one who did not bear some mark of the process of violent change: Bandages, bruises, and limps were the rule.

At the Lyceum Building I proceeded with the long-delayed business of registering as a student at the University of Mississippi. We entered through the rear. Fortunately at the time I did not know that it was the back door; otherwise, I would have had to confront the question of whether this was a concession to the Mississippi "way of life."

James Meredith arrives for registration at the University of Mississippi, Monday, October 1, 1962.

(Photo by Ed Meek courtesy Department of Archives and Special Collections, University of Mississippi)

It was a dismal day. Even the newsmen were spiritless. Behind a desk Robert B. Ellis, the Registrar, was waiting. He was the lone stand-out, the only man on the scene with spirit—a spirit of defiance, of contempt if not hatred. Doar stated our purpose. The Registrar presented me with forms, and I filled out all but one—my class schedule form. As I studied it, obviously Ellis knew what was on my mind. One course on my schedule was a duplicate of one with the same title, which I had already completed with the grade of A. Later when I arrived at the class I found that the instructor was using the very same textbook.

Registrar Robert B. Ellis admitting James Meredith
Source unknown

Ellis said, "Meredith—" (He was the only official at the university who did not address me with the usual title of courtesy.) "—you may as well sign."

I tried to discuss the duplicate course with him, but it was no use. I decided to take the matter up through other channels. The schedule was later changed to suit my needs.

I signed and we left the room. The press had been patient. I consented to stop and make a statement though there was not much to ask and even less to say. The first question was, "Now that you are finally registered, are you happy?" I could only express my true feeling that, "This is no happy occasion." Truly, it was no time for joy.

On my way out of the Lyceum Building, I encountered my first Negro. What would his reaction be? What would our relationship be? What would be our communication? He had his cleaning tools—as all Negroes on the campus must keep them visible.

Under one arm was a broom. As I walked past he acted as if he had not noticed anything unusual. Then he touched me with the handle of his broom and caught my eye. I got the message. Every Negro on the campus was on my team and would be watching out for me at the University of Mississippi. Later on, I got to know this fellow very well. He told me that he just had to let me know that they were with me. To bump me with the broom handle was the best way he could think of to communicate with me.

At nine o'clock I attended my first class, Colonial American History. I was a few minutes late and was assigned a seat at the back of the room. The professor was lecturing on conditions in England at the time of the colonization of America. He pretended to pay no special attention when I entered. When U.S. marshals started to follow me, however, he asked them to remain outside. This precedent was maintained during my entire stay at the university.

I think there were about a dozen students in class. One said hello to me and the others were silent. I remember a girl—the only girl there, I think—began crying. But it might have been from the tear gas in the room. I was tearing up from it myself.

I had three classes scheduled that day. I went to two. The third did not meet because there was too much tear gas in the room.

This day, October 1, 1962, was a turning point in my three years in Mississippi. The first phase—to breach the system of "White Supremacy"—had been accomplished. Although I only had a toehold in the door, the solid wall had been breached.

After attending the classes, the return up the hill to Baxter Hall also marked a turning point in my personal struggle in the fight for human freedom and dignity. I felt a sudden release of pressure that I perhaps cannot put into words. I remarked to John Doar about this feeling of relief. He did not seem to understand. Perhaps this was not the time for philosophizing, I thought, since I was the only one who had gotten any rest the previous night. But I had the feeling that my personal battle was over. The pressure from inner doubt, always present in one's mind, that one's best might not be good enough, was gone. The often-debated question of whether or not I would break under the constant pressure no longer troubled my mind.

To me, the ultimate outcome was relatively insignificant. Whether or not I went on to graduate was a minor issue. The important thing was that I had earned the privilege of choice. At the time I was aware that Negroes recognized only "Success" and "Titles," and I had bypassed the degree-title several times, knowing full well that if I should fail in this effort, I would be soon forgotten. However, as we slowly ascended the hill toward Baxter Hall, it appeared to me that the steps I had chosen to carry out the mandate of my Divine Responsibility had been proper and timely.

James Meredith is an American civil rights activist, writer and Air Force veteran. His books include *Three Years in Mississippi* and *A Mission from God*. A native of Kosciusko, Mississippi, Meredith joined the military after high school and attended Jackson State University before becoming the first African-American student to attend the University of Mississippi in 1962. After graduating from Ole Miss in 1963 Meredith attended Columbia Law School, attained a law degree and became involved in politics.

Assignment: Mississippi
by Dorothy Gilliam
from *Trailblazers: A Pioneering Journalist's Fight
to Make the Media Look More Like America*,
New York: Center Street, 2019
(reprinted with permission)

Dorothy Gilliam
(Photo by Kea Dupree Photography)

James Meredith's integration of Ole Miss took thirty-two thousand federal troops to enroll him, and two people were killed on the campus in the insurrection that followed his enrollment. I couldn't imagine Meredith's situation! Beyond the fear for his life, I imagined Meredith's loneliness, not having white friends to demystify Ole Miss or Black friends to sustain him and counter the white supremacy he had come to fight.

I was thrilled that my people were ripping off the manacles of segregation all over the South. Yet, when I heard the news of Meredith's suit, my Southern upbringing made it hard for me to believe he was taking such a bold and dangerous course. I remarked to friends, "A lone Black man trying to integrate that bastion of white supremacy? Meredith must be very brave—or crazy!" When I later got to know him, I learned he was shrewd, disciplined, independent-minded and incredibly courageous. I did not know at the time that Meredith filed suit that I would soon be covering a part of the story about his hard-won integration of the university.

Meredith was a native Mississippian who had served nine years in the U.S. Air Force and studied a year and a half at Jackson State College, a Black institution. He was born on an eighty-four-acre farm in Kosciusko, Mississippi, and lived there until he left to spend his senior year in high school in Florida and then serve in the U.S. Air Force, much of that time in Japan. He was twenty-six, married, and the father of a six-month-old son when he returned in 1960, in his own words, to "fight a war." He wanted to attack what he considered "the Negroes' worst enemy: the principles and doctrine of 'White Supremacy.' "

When Meredith enrolled in Jackson State College, he entered as an advanced junior. There he found a group of intellectuals who became his support group in his daring goal to get a degree from the University of Mississippi—the state's flagship university. He was encouraged by the way President Eisenhower had intervened in the 1959 integration of Little Rock's Central High School. Meredith said he felt the election of President Kennedy provided the proper atmosphere for the inevitable struggle between the state and the federal government that his application would prompt. He wrote the University of Mississippi seeking an application on January 21, 1961, the day after Kennedy's inauguration. The university twice denied him admission, but the veteran's action was destined to spark the greatest constitutional crisis since the Civil War.

For months, Meredith and his lawyers traveled across Mississippi, often followed by state government investigators, pursuing their legal fight, while state officials retaliated with a battle plan of obstruction, evasion, and delay. The case eventually went to the U.S. Supreme Court, which ruled in Meredith's favor on September 10, 1962.

Chief U.S. Marshal James McShane (left) and federal attorney
John Doar (right) escort James Meredith on campus
*(Photo by Ed Meek courtesy Department of Archives and Special Collections,
University of Mississippi)*

Mississippi Governor Ross Barnett led state officials in defying
the courts and the U.S. government, fueling his state's rebellion
in a stand that delighted most white Mississippians. On the
afternoon of September 20, with Meredith enroute to Oxford,
the university's panic-stricken board of trustees voted to dodge the
crisis by appointing Governor Barnett "temporary registrar" of the
university. When Meredith and escorts from the U.S. Marshal's
Office arrived for his first attempt to enroll, about two thousand
protesters, some shouting, "Go home, n----r," greeted him.
Governor Barnett personally denied him admittance.

The U.S. government bucked this direct challenge to its
authority in federal court. Barnett issued a proclamation declaring
the federal government's action a "direct usurpation" of state
power— invoking the invalid doctrine of interposition. A closely
watched contempt trial followed, and state education officials
promised to permit Meredith to register.

On his second try, officials told Meredith he had to register in
Jackson in the Woolfolk State Office Building with the university's
board of trustees. When Meredith and federal officials arrived to
register him, a crowd of some two thousand white people taunted

him, and Meredith was again turned away. As Meredith departed, some in the crowd shouted that Ross, not Attorney General Robert F. Kennedy, was "the big boss." On September 26, when Meredith and his U.S. Marshal escorts traveled to the Oxford campus so he could try to enroll for the third time. Lieutenant Governor Paul Johnson turned him away from the entrance to the campus. Cited for contempt, top Mississippi officials refused to appear in the U.S. District Court in New Orleans for the trial. The frustrated judges responded that it was up to the U.S. government to act.

Robert Kennedy, who had been orchestrating events from Washington, D.C., as the nation's chief law enforcement officer, thought he had an agreement with Barnett to enroll Meredith the next day, September 27. However, as the motorcade bearing Meredith was making the ninety-mile drive from Meredith's safe house in Memphis to Oxford, the plan fell apart, and Meredith's caravan turned around—failing in his fourth attempt to enroll.

Meanwhile, Oxford was descending into anarchy as word spread that Meredith would soon be returning to the campus. Ku Klux Klansmen were relaying information to the imperial wizard at his Alabama headquarters. White Citizens' Council members mingled in the crowd. Some people brazenly walked the streets with their guns in plain sight. A mob numbering some 2,500 people gathered around the campus.

The fifth attempt to register Meredith would be on Monday, October 1. On the day before, Sunday, September 30, a hastily organized federal protection force made up of 123 deputy marshals led by Assistant Attorney General Nicholas Katzenbach, 316 border policemen, and 97 federal prison guards was deployed to the Ole Miss campus in anticipation of Meredith's arrival.

Wearing gas masks, helmets, and vests with pockets for tear gas canisters, the marshals lined up outside the Lyceum Building where Meredith would go to register that Monday. The crowd cursed the stoic marshals and called them n----r lovers. Oxford radio stations began announcing that the federal government had taken over the university, prompting hundreds more people to descend on the campus.

Robert Kennedy successfully worked out a secret plan with a

reluctantly compliant Governor Barnett. As dusk fell that Sunday evening, Meredith slipped unnoticed with his escorts onto the campus through a side entrance and moved into his dormitory, Baxter Hall. The goal was for him to register the next day as the first African American student at Ole Miss. Twenty-four federal agents guarded the hallway outside his room with a standing order to kill anyone who threatened Meredith's safety.

As word spread that Meredith was on the campus, intense rioting by whites broke out on the circle in front of the Lyceum Building, where marshals stood, and the usually staid campus became a battle scene. At one point, the mob started hurling bottles at the dormitory where Meredith was, and federal officials monitoring events from Washington panicked. "You don't want to have a lynching," JFK aide Kenneth O' Donnell was quoted as saying. The U.S. marshals and Mississippi National Guard held the bloodthirsty mob at bay into the wee hours. By morning, two people had been killed execution-style by the white mob, a French journalist, Paul Guihard, and a twenty-three-year-old white curiosity seeker, Ray Gunter. More than seventy others were injured. President Kennedy went on national television and announced to the nation he would send in federal troops, tens of thousands of troops in all, to make certain Meredith would be enrolled.

(Photo by Ed Meek courtesy Department of Archives and Special Collections, University of Mississippi)

People often ask why Black people in Mississippi didn't fight back when the white segregationists rioted on the campus of the university. Fear was a factor. The small Black population in Oxford were mostly service workers at the university. While some doubtless owned guns to protect their families, even the bravest would be afraid to fight against such

21

overwhelming odds. MPs patrolled the Oxford Square the Klan walked about displaying guns. Black people had no power and no vote in Mississippi, nor in most other Southern states.

On October 1, Meredith successfully enrolled in the university, and shortly after the news reached Washington, Ben Gilbert, *The Washington Post's* city editor, walked over to my desk and asked me to come with him to the office of Al Friendly, the managing editor, in another part of the newsroom. Al asked me to sit down, and Ben told me they wanted me to go to Oxford and other sites in Mississippi. They wanted me to interview Black leaders across the state for their reactions and to write about the African American community's response to these historic events.

I had been working at The Washington Post for twelve months and married for one month. In the days before this assignment, I had watched with the rest of the world, feeling angry and helpless to do much about it. By going to Mississippi, I could at least write about it. Although I knew I would have to report objectively about what 1 found, I had felt a deep anger at Mississippi's rebellion and the way Meredith was being treated, and I rejoiced at the chance to report from the scene. I would write a major piece for *The Washington Post's* weekly "think" section called Outlook, over which Friendly, as managing editor, presided. 1 would also contribute news stories from Oxford, depending on what my reporting uncovered.

It was encouraging that Ben realized I was a special resource for the paper—someone with whom Black Mississippians would talk honestly and share deep feelings. However, I wasn't the first Black reporter the newspaper had sent south. Wallace H. Terry had been hired in 1960 and traveled to the South often, one of the few Negroes working the civil rights beat for a mainstream daily. He later joined *Washington Post* reporter Robert E. Lee Baker in covering Alabama Governor George Wallace's defiance against integration at the University of Alabama in 1963. I was nervous about going to Mississippi, where Black life was considered cheap as dirt. White supremacy's legal and political framework was established at a Mississippi constitutional convention in 1890 that excluded Blacks from voting and that was maintained through violence and lynching. From 1882 to 1927, 517 Blacks were lynched in the state—the highest number in the nation for any state during that period.

I had always looked at Mississippi as a place apart. James Meredith was risking death. I was afraid but kept my fears to myself and accepted the assignment with a degree of confidence, because I would have a secret weapon—I intended to hire Ernest Withers, a freelance photographer, to take pictures for me. I knew he was experienced and savvy in dealing with the threats, dangers, and violence of Mississippi. I had worked with Withers while at *The Tri-State Defender*, most notably traveling with him to Little Rock in 1957 during the integration crisis at Central High School. I had later used him as a photographer when 1 was an associate editor at *JET* magazine from late 1957 to August 1959. 1 knew he had seven sons and a daughter. He often joked with me that I had something in common with his wife. Her name was also Dorothy.

I was so excited about the opportunity to go to Oxford that it didn't occur to me to protest to Ben and Al that I didn't know where I would stay when I got there. I presumed the tiny town of 6,200 residents had no hotels or motels for Blacks, but I figured Withers would help me find sleeping arrangements somewhere. As a Washington Post reporter, I had a reasonable expense account and was happy to provide Withers with per diem pay and expenses, plus the cost of any photographs the paper used. 1 hadn't had those kinds of funds when Withers accompanied me to Little Rock.

Withers was a double asset because he knew his way around the South, including how to comport himself around white Southerners. He was a quick-talking former policeman who learned photography in the army and loved taking pictures. He took some of the most iconic photographs of the Civil Rights Movement. Some of his photographs hang in the National Civil Rights Museum in Memphis, and his work has appeared in many books about the movement. I felt privileged to work with him and protected from some of the dangers of covering the segregated South.

The Washington Post had been covering the daily breaking news about Ole Miss in detail. The newspaper had reorganized its staff to cover the Civil Rights Movement after the Supreme Court passed its unanimous decision to outlaw public school segregation across the nation. The executive editor, J. Russell Wiggins, and Al Friendly put the city editor in charge of school desegregation and civil rights coverage, even though it had national as well as local and regional impact.

Gilbert had hired Robert E. Lee Baker away from the Fredericksburg, Virginia, *Free Lance-Star*, and he had been covering the beat for several years by the fall of 1961, when I arrived at *The Washington Post*. According to Chalmers Roberts, Gilbert had given these instructions to Baker; "You've got to forget that you're white and are dealing with Negroes. Adopt a different skin color—have a green skin. Write so that both Negroes and whites will understand what you are talking about."

Baker's enterprise reporting on the news pages had yielded big results. He covered the Montgomery bus boycott and first introduced *Washington Post* readers to a "27-year-old Negro pastor of the Dexter Avenue Baptist Church and an active NAACP member"—Dr. King. Baker had covered some racial issues in Virginia as its legislature fought to preserve segregation. In 1958, Baker had reported from Dawson, Georgia, where white authorities and others were brutalizing and terrorizing Negro residents. Baker quoted Sheriff Z. T. (Zeke) Matthews: "You know. Cap', there's nothing like fear to keep the n----rs in line. I believe we ought to be strict about who votes."

As a Southerner, 1 knew Mississippi was a land of Black death, but 1 went there anyway. When I received this possible last assignment one year into my job at *The Washington Post*, not only was I just twenty-four and newly married but, unbeknown to me, I was already pregnant. My husband Sam, a native Mississippian although raised in Louisville from age seven, expressed concern for my safety because he knew the dangers firsthand. He was fearful, but he realized it was an assignment that I could not pass up, even if I had the choice. I knew it was dangerous, too, from my experience five years earlier, when I had covered the Little Rock Nine when I worked at *The Tri-State Defender*.

I flew to Memphis to meet Withers on October 2, 1962, the day after Meredith enrolled. I arrived in the late afternoon, and we soon set out in his car down U.S. 51 to drive the ninety miles to Oxford. Dusk was beginning to fall, and the roads felt eerie. Just before we got to Batesville, Mississippi, on a two-lane country road, I noticed that a pickup truck with gun racks on the roof was tailing us. The men in the truck signaled for us to pull over by waving their arms. They pulled in front of us. Withers pulled over. It was dark by then, and I wondered if they were stopping us not only because we were Black but also because Withers's car had out-of-state (Tennessee) license plates. Two menacing-looking men walked slowly and threateningly to the driver's side. "Where y'all n-----s going?" one asked. They weren't huge men, but they looked strong enough to do some harm. In the darkness, I couldn't see if they actually had guns. These white men, who were not connected with any law enforcement, knew any white could stop any Blacks for any reason.

"To Jackson, to see my cousin," answered Withers, who had packed his cameras away in the trunk where he always kept them when he drove south, so as not to arouse suspicion.

"Get goin' then, and make sure you steer clear of Oxford," the other one said.

Ernest said, "Yassuh," and drove away. My heart was in my mouth as Withers drove down several dark side roads, taking an alternate route to get to Oxford.

The radio had been reporting that unreconstructed rebels, White Citizens' Council hardliners and various other segregationists from across the nation had descended on Mississippi to help repel the federal takeover in an insurrection that some said was like a replay of the Civil War.

The fighting continued raging earlier October 1 a few blocks from the campus even as Meredith was registering. Former army general Edwin Walker, a right-wing fanatic, had gone on the radio publicly pleading for volunteers to help repel the "Federals." Some of these volunteers had rioted at Ole Miss the previous night, and others kept arriving the next morning and setting up positions at Courthouse Square and beyond.

Mississippi highway patrolmen stood by doing nothing, one saying their orders were "not to interfere." Federal officials

25

intervened. A thousand men of the Second Infantry Division's Second Battle Group, wearing bulletproof flak jackets, had arrived from Fort Benning, Georgia, as I was preparing to fly out of Washington, D.C. It was an integrated group, almost one-third Black, and as they marched to the Square, the furious rioters taunted the Black and white soldiers and threw bottles at them. Meanwhile, more troops were pouring into Mississippi.

As we drove, Withers told me that he and Larry Still, a dogged reporter from *JET* magazine, had interviewed and photographed Meredith the first time he had tried to enroll. I knew Larry from my two-year employment at "the little magazine that could." Withers said Still and he had followed the caravan of marshals and state highway patrolmen in a rental car from Memphis and, when the motorcade stopped, got to take some pictures. Withers said the two of them followed the entourage all the way to Oxford but weren't permitted on campus. "We got the hell outa there!" said Withers, who took their being barred as a frightening harbinger of what might lie ahead.

Most of the Black reporters and photographers, who with rare exceptions were still employed only by the Black press, couldn't get into good positions to cover the story in Oxford.

Moses Newson of the Baltimore *Afro-American* (opposite) and Jimmy Hicks (below) of *The New York Amsterdam News*, both of whom I had met covering Little Rock five years earlier, were denied access and proximity to the campus and covered most of the story from Memphis. A story buried deep in The Afro carried this disclosure, "Colored newspapermen on the scene are being kept away from the campus of the university." After Meredith registered on  October 1 and thousands of troops were in place, Black reporters could finally report from the campus.

Oxford Police Chief Jimmy Jones questioning Amsterdam News
executive editor James Hicks (far right).
*(Photo by Ed Meek courtesy Department of Archives and Special Collections,
University of Mississippi)*

By the time Withers and I arrived in Oxford on Tuesday, October 2, the smell of tear gas was still in the air as thousands of army troops were keeping peace on the campus. At night, soldiers slept in tents on a hillside behind the campus. The next day, it was safe for us to drive onto the campus that still bore the marks of the "Battle of Ole Miss" two nights before. We saw Molotov cocktails, dead squirrels (that had been overcome by tear gas), a smoldering vehicle, and bricks strewn about. I took special note of the Negro soldiers in the background. Initially Black soldiers were on the front lines, but they were later pulled back when they became targets of the mobs.

I was in a battle zone and felt much tension.

1 didn't attempt to interview James Meredith in Baxter Hall, the huge dormitory he occupied alone, except for his U.S. Marshal escorts and guards. Let the Black and white reporters covering breaking news do that. I was focusing on the reaction of Blacks on the streets of Oxford and across the state to this breakthrough in civil rights. I wanted to know what difference Meredith's military-backed admission had made in the lives of other Black

Mississippians. My mission was out in the town, where the people lived, and I felt a wave of relief as we left the campus through the front entrance.

Harder than finding the story, however, would be locating a place to stay. I knew Mississippi's white hotels and motels wouldn't rent me a room, and I could risk my life by even trying them. Black reporters working the Southern beat for Black newspapers had faced this problem for years. Black journalists shared all the problems of white reporters—as a largely Northern antagonistic press confronting fiercely hostile white populations—but in addition, we faced the actual circumstances of segregation; we could not check into a hotel, eat in restaurants, use public restrooms, or drink from water fountains as the white journalists did. At highly covered civil rights trials, such as that for the murder of Emmett Till, ample space was set up for white reporters, while the "Negro press table" was a folding card table not large enough to accommodate the Black reporters. Describing it in his book *Shocking the Conscience: A Reporter's Account of the Civil Rights Movement,* Simeon Booker called it the Jim Crow table.

When I worked at *JET,* I admired reporters like Booker, Francis H. Mitchell, and Mark Crawford, who risked their lives for years to tell readers about the struggle for freedom in the South. Moses Newson of *The Afro-American* was fearless and dedicated as he traveled to Southern hot spots. He suffered burns when a bomb exploded on the bus he was on with the Freedom Riders. "You prepare to go south like you prepare to go to war," he once told me.

The racial obstacles would be no different for me or the handful of other Blacks working for the white press. When Carl Rowan covered the dramatic struggle to integrate Little Rock's Central High School for *The Minneapolis Tribune,* he sometimes stayed with Daisy Bates, the mentor of the Little Rock Nine, and her husband, L. C. Bates, as did the other Black reporters. Rowan later said, "This was a pleasure and a great journalistic advantage— until the racists began shooting through the Bates' window and dropping an occasional homemade bomb. During my late-in-the-crisis visits, we would put lights around the house and sit up all night playing poker, utterly afraid to go to sleep." Rowan recalled these experiences in his book *Breaking Barriers*.

I had also stayed at the Bates' house when 1 went to Little Rock. In later years, I realized that as a woman, I was even more vulnerable than the Black men were when segregation forced me to stay in the home of strangers just to do my job. I often felt only divine protection kept me from being molested in those situations. Who knew what kind of "sleepwalkers" might be around these houses at night? I was afraid at times but had learned to be courageous when working in the Deep South war zone.

In Oxford, the white reporters could comfortably bed down in hotels, dine in the restaurants or order room service, and sit in the lobby trading stories with their peers. Not so for Withers and me. Our first night there, Withers suggested we find a Black funeral home because he knew they were valuable sources of information and might suggest a home in which I might lodge. Every Black community had one. It was late when we arrived at Oxford's only Black funeral home and met the owner and director, G. W. Bankhead. Withers found other quarters, but I was grateful to stay at the mortuary—in a spare room in the family quarters upstairs from where bodies were received and prepared for burial. 1 was glad for a clean, safe place to lay my head and to have found a Black establishment that would get me closer to my story. Black funeral directors were the go-to people for information for Black reporters.

That night, I heard the noise of people's voices in the house, and in the morning, I learned the body of a young Black man had been brought in in the wee hours—not unusual at a funeral home. With whites engaging in bloody rioting on the campus, I suspected foul play—a fear that the funeral director did not corroborate, so I neither investigated nor reported it. Twenty-five years later when I repeated my suspicion at a forum for journalists at the twenty-fifth anniversary of the integration of Ole Miss, a white Mississippian told me that no killing of a young Black man had occurred during the siege of "Ole Miss."

In the morning, Withers and I got directions to Freedman's Town, the neighborhood where most Blacks lived. I set out to survey some of Oxford's Blacks for their reaction to Meredith's heroic feat, and I easily found people to interview there. I introduced myself as a reporter from *The Washington Post*, but I'm not certain many knew it was the second-largest paper in the nation.

People were welcoming and talked openly even if they were surprised to see a young colored woman from a white newspaper. In fact, I found them eager to talk to me. Reporters from the white, rabidly segregationist Mississippi papers that Blacks saw as the enemy never interviewed them. Northern reporters were mainly interested in Governor Barnett and the Meredith drama on campus. Some Black Oxford citizens said mobs attacked them as they tried to report to the university for their service jobs— as maids, janitors, drivers, servers, and cooks. Mobs pulled them from their cars, smashed their window's, and otherwise heaped a stream of violence on them.

Bill Mayes, a member of the army's 503d Military Police Battalion, told others that on the second and third days of the occupation, so much fear spread through the Freedman's Town area that he found Black families up in the surrounding hills, huddled together, camping. "They had abandoned their homes and gone up to the forests with tents. We found them in the woods," he said.

The Black people I interviewed had *not* run for the hills. They were shocked and amazed by Meredith's courage and overjoyed by his determination to integrate the university.

I wrote my first story about the community when we left Oxford and arrived in Jackson, Mississippi, where I was able to check into a Black motel. I felt safer there because Jackson was more urban, with Black churches, businesses, and a significant black population. When I worked at *JET*, reporters on the Southern race beat had shared stories of how in the 1930s, reporters for Black newspapers would steal into town by bus at night to avoid the Klansmen. Some reporters would wear overalls and muddy shoes to disguise themselves. They would carry their wobbly Royal portable typewriter wrapped in brown paper so it would look like a pack of clothes. Even in the 1950s and 1960s, Black journalists carried Bibles to look like preachers or had false credentials in case local authorities became suspicious of their roles.

With a Jackson, Mississippi, dateline, the first story I wrote was headlined, "Mississippi Negroes Happily Stunned by Meredith," and appeared on the front page of *The Washington Post* on October 6:

> *The hot sun glistened on the young Negro lawyer's face as he lolled in a seat by his office window. He was reminiscing about his first racial jolt—at age 6.*
>
> *"I went into a store to buy a coke and the storekeeper yelled at me. 'Put it back! We don't sell no Cokes to no n----rs on Sunday!'"*
>
> *He chuckled as he recalled the merchant's assurance that he could have an orange or a grape, however, for his same sweaty nickel.*
>
> *"The episode," the lawyer said, pointed out for him what has long been the rule in Mississippi: "Negroes get pretty much what whites want them to have."*
>
> *Many Mississippi Negroes say Meredith's entry into "Ole Miss," in the face of Gov. Ross Barnett's sworn resistance to Federal court orders, was an accomplishment of the impossible. It was the crack in the thick wall of segregation that may someday broaden, they say, so Negroes themselves may choose—and get— what they want.*

I returned from Oxford with enough information to file my main story for *The Washington Post's* weekly Outlook section and was pleased when Al Friendly put it on the front of the prestigious section on October 14, beneath the headline "Mississippi Mood: Hope and Fear." It read:

> *Hope and fear are the moods of Negroes in Mississippi these anxious days.*
>
> *You can spot these feelings in the hesitant words of a disenfranchised Negro handyman in Oxford who hobbles heavily to a chair, hikes up his overalls, and talks.*
>
> *Or in the bold words of a harassed Negro leader [Medgar Evers] who, despite constant danger, declares that James H. Meredith's entry into the University of Mississippi "is a clear breakthrough" for Negroes and will be a springboard for other advances.*
>
> *"The hope is that Meredith signals the coming of the light for all of them. The fear is that the inevitable changes will bring further death, destruction, and repercussions.*

Dorothy Gilliam was born in Memphis, Tennessee. In 1957 she became a reporter for the Memphis *Tri-State Defender*. She later worked at *JET* and *Ebony*. In 1961 she earned a master's Degree at Columbia University and was hired by *The Washington Post* when she was 24, the first African-American woman to be hired as a reporter by the paper. In 2010 the Washington Press Club awarded Gilliam its lifetime achievement award.

The Warrior
By William Doyle

from *An American Insurrection: James Meredith and the Battle of Oxford, Mississippi, 1962.* New York: Anchor Books/Random House, 2001.
(used with permission)

William Doyle
(Photograph by Enrique Shore)

James Howard Meredith is a character so colorful and complex, he could only have sprung from the rich soil of Mississippi. He seemed to dwell inside a myth of his own design, a realm often remote and impenetrable to other people. He was an obscure loner who before his thirtieth birthday would engineer a stunning historical coup by mobilizing thousands of people to do his will, including the president and the Supreme Court of the United States. He was a supremely logical man whose reasoning would be misunderstood by practically everyone, a brilliant strategist who would be dismissed by many as being crazy. His sudden impact on Mississippi history would pack the explosive power of a social and political bombshell.

James Meredith is an intense, slightly built man of five feet seven inches, with piercing eyes. He was born in the heart of central Mississippi's hilly farm country in a place called Kosciusko, a town named for a Polish freedom fighter in the American Revolution. People who met him often found him an enigmatic, even mystical personality. "If I know what a mystic is, then James Meredith is a mystic," reported David Sansing, a University of Mississippi history professor. "He doesn't think like we do, he doesn't act like we do, he doesn't even hear the same sounds we hear." Historian Arthur Schlesinger, Jr., described Meredith simply as "a lonely, taciturn and quixotic man of courage and purpose."

Meredith boasted of a dazzling array of ancestors. Some of them seemed in symbolic collision with one another and even themselves, and some may have been connected to Meredith more in myth than physical reality. He claimed one great-great-grandfather who was crown prince of the African kingdom of Dahomey; and a Native-American great-grandfather, General Sam Cobb. "My great-grandfather was the national leader of the Choctaw nation when it was dissolved," Meredith said of Cobb in a 2000 interview, "and that was why I always wanted to be a general. For twenty years he was in every major war against the Indians with General [Andrew] Jackson on Jackson's side."

Meredith also traced his lineage to a white great-grandfather, Judge J. A. P. Campbell, a colonel in the Confederate army who later, as Mississippi Supreme Court justice, helped write the notorious white-supremacist 1890 state constitution. "Campbell was my father's mother's father," reported Meredith. "He had a white family and a Black family. He spent the last twenty-seven years of his life with his Black family. It was really not an uncommon thing in those days. He practically raised my father."

The most regal figure in Meredith's life was his father, Moses Meredith, a proud, fiercely independent farmer, the son of a slave, who, unlike the great majority of Mississippi Blacks, was both a property holder and a registered voter. His commanding presence generated respect from everyone, especially James, who called his father Cap, short for "Captain." "Everything I have ever done in my life," Meredith explained, "has been a direct result of what my father taught me. I have continued on his mission."

Mississippi was a semi-sovereign empire of white supremacy, but Cap Meredith ran his eighty-five-acre property like a free and independent kingdom inside it. He and his wife, Roxie, steered all ten of their children through high school, and seven into college. Cap fenced off the family's property from neighboring white farms and minimized contact with outsiders, both Black and white. "We were most isolated," said Meredith. "Our relationship with people Black and white was totally controlled by my father." It was Cap Meredith's way of infusing pride and self-sufficiency in his children.

As a boy, young James Meredith roamed the fields and streams to catch grasshoppers and crickets to sell to fishermen as bait, and after school he plowed the fields with his father. At night sometimes he built a city in his dreams. He never could figure out where the city was, but he knew it was light-years from Kosciusko. When he was around twelve, he visited a white doctor's office and gazed up at a picture of the doctor as a star football player at the University of Mississippi. Meredith then had a young boy's dream of attending the football-powerhouse school himself.

Meredith didn't fully comprehend the gulf between the races until he was fifteen, when his family drove north to visit relatives. James took the train back with his brother. "The train wasn't segregated when we left Detroit," Meredith recalled in 1962, "but when we got to Memphis the conductor told my brother and me we had to go to another car. I cried all the way home from Memphis, and in a way I have cried ever since."

Meredith was among the first wave of Black soldiers to serve in the racially integrated U.S. armed forces—he enlisted directly out of high school in 1951, just three years after Harry Truman's historic 1948 desegregation order. Meredith selected the Air Force because as a brand-new service branch formed after the war, it had no legacy of racism to overcome and had the best reputation among Blacks for fair treatment. Meredith thought the desegregation of the military was among the most epochal developments in the history of Black Americans.

Meredith was now in his sixth year in the Air Force, where he worked his way up as a clerk typist. He was known for being extremely meticulous, well organized, and frugal. He was said to grab unused typing paper out of the wastebasket to avoid wasting resources. In 1956 Meredith married Mary June Wiggins of Gary, Indiana, and she followed him to his posting in Japan. He planned to return to Mississippi after his final military hitch to study law, but his experience as a Black noncommissioned American officer in Japan was a transforming one.

In the United States, Meredith always felt conscious of his racial identity. But Japan felt like another world. "Japan is where I got it all together as a man," recalled Meredith. He was amazed by the air of racial tolerance he experienced in the Japan of the mid-1950s, which was just emerging from American-occupation rule and was consumed with re-industrializing at a furious pace. "I never felt as free as in Japan," he declared. "You were first and foremost an American."

The racial turmoil of his home country, however, was rarely far from Meredith's heart. He had always been an intense student of race relations and spent many hours of anguish during his military service following the news of racial strife at home, to the point of developing stomach trouble. "I don't ever want to think I am 'well adjusted' as a Negro," he once quipped. When Meredith appeared before a military promotion board in 1954, rather than asking him about his job responsibilities, the colonels asked him his opinion of the recent Supreme Court decision ordering the desegregation of public schools in the United States. He told them in no uncertain terms of his support, and after they promoted him to staff sergeant, the colonels told him they were with him in the struggle but "the outcome will depend on you." From then on Meredith considered that statement a personal badge of responsibility.

In September 1957 when he was in the U.S. Air Force and stationed in Japan, Meredith met a young Japanese schoolboy and the two began chatting about the Little Rock crisis, which had been given wide coverage in Japan. The boy was stunned to meet someone from Mississippi and couldn't believe that Meredith would want to go back to such a place. The encounter helped persuade Meredith that he should someday go back to his home state to fight for a better society.

In Mississippi, Meredith thought, the state system of white

supremacy was so powerful and violent that traditional civil disobedience was doomed to ineffectiveness. "I really thought they were crazy," he later said about the tactics of the traditional civil rights movement when applied to his homeland. "I mean, they were out of their minds. Anyone talking about going into Mississippi and dealing with a strategy of nonviolence, turning the other cheek, I think, these people got to be crazy."

Now, as the 101st Airborne patrolled the streets of Little Rock, Meredith speculated that white supremacy in his own state might be overthrown, but only if confronted with such overwhelming physical force and firepower.

"Little Rock," Meredith explained in a 2000 interview, "was a very, very big factor in my whole desire to break the system of white supremacy. I genuinely believed that the only way that we would get our full rights of citizenship was to get a greater military force on our side than Mississippi had, and there was only one force in the world bigger than that, and that was the U.S. armed forces. So when Eisenhower, who had been the biggest general in our history, committed the troops to support the rights of citizenship, that was what my objective was in the whole Mississippi scheme."

In July 1960 James Meredith was honorably discharged from the Air Force. He returned to Mississippi and registered for the fall semester at all-Black Jackson State College, in the state capital of Jackson, to complete his studies toward a bachelor's degree in political science. The school was a showpiece in the state's failing public-relations campaign to deliver education for Blacks that was "separate but equal." Meredith might as well have landed on another planet. Until now, he had lived mostly in societies where white supremacy was irrelevant: a childhood in the isolated independence of his father's farm; nine years in the integrated U.S. Air Force; and three of those years stationed in Japan, where the concept of white supremacy was nonexistent. Suddenly Meredith was in the belly of the most segregated state in the nation, a society that one local white newspaper editor called a "jungle of hate."

At the dawn of the 1960s, Mississippi was both the poorest state in the country, with annual per capita income of just $1,233, and the state with the highest proportion of Black citizens, approximately

43 percent. Radical white segregationists controlled the police, the media, and the state government; dominated the hearts and minds of much of the white population; and systematically eradicated the citizenship rights of Black residents.

If you were Black in Mississippi in 1960, the overwhelming odds were that you could not vote, could not hold office or serve on a jury, suffered substandard schools and housing, and were totally segregated from normal American life. There were no Black sheriffs, state Highway Patrolmen or National Guardsmen. The token number of twenty-two thousand Black voters in 1952 was beaten down by violence and terrorist threats to eight thousand in 1958. Racial violence against Blacks, by white citizens and police forces alike, was a matter of established routine, especially when Blacks attempted to organize politically.

Medgar Evers
(Britannca.com)

A daring young Black army veteran named Medgar Evers was in his seventh year as field secretary of the state NAACP, working with courageous Black leaders such as Aaron Henry of Clarksdale, C. C. Bryant of McComb, and Amzie Moore of Cleveland, Mississippi. Acting as a one-man intelligence agency, Evers donned disguises to dash around the state investigating atrocities against Black citizens. His wife and assistant, Myrlie Evers, reported that "affidavits testifying to the routine cruelty of white Mississippians toward Negroes piled up in Medgar's files. Each represented an hour, a day, a week of Medgar's life in a surrealist version of Hell."

The reports wove a monotonous montage of horror. In the Delta town of Belzoni on May 7, 1955, a Baptist minister and NAACP member named Rev. George Washington Lee was executed by gunshots to the head soon after he registered to vote. Three months later, Lamar Smith, a sixty-year-old Black farmer who registered to vote and encouraged others to join him, was assassinated by gunfire in broad daylight on the courthouse lawn of Brookhaven. That August also brought the kidnapping, beating, and execution of young Emmett Till, an act so heinous it triggered worldwide revulsion.

There seemed to be no end to the nightmare. Reports of beatings and intimidation kept piling up in Medgar Evers's office. In 1958 Woodrow Wilson Daniels died of a brain injury after being beaten by a white sheriff, who was tried and acquitted. The next year, in Poplarville, Mack Charles Parker was charged with raping a white woman, dragged from jail, and shot to death by a mob, his body dumped into the Pearl River. In October 1959, Luther Jackson was shot to death by a policeman in Philadelphia, Mississippi. No charges were filed.

"A map of Mississippi," recalled Mrs. Evers, "was a reminder not of geography, but of atrocities, of rivers that hid broken bodies, of towns and cities ruled by the enemy."

Elsewhere in the United States, as the new decade began, African-Americans were beginning to challenge white supremacy with creative new tactics and mounting excitement. As the old-line NAACP continued to press legal assaults on Southern segregation, younger groups such as the Congress of Racial Equality (CORE) and the Reverend Martin Luther King, Jr.'s, Southern Christian Leadership Conference (SCLC) planned grass-roots action. In February 1960 four Black college students in Greensboro, North Carolina, were refused service at a Woolworth's lunch counter, and their tactic of staying put until they were served triggered a wave of "sit-ins" and "pray-ins" around the country.

As a student at all-Black Jackson State, James Meredith sharpened his growing political consciousness by helping to form a small secret society of campus intellectuals called the Mississippi Improvement Association of Students, or MIAS. Their weapon was the mimeograph machine, and their ammunition was leaflets announcing they were going to break the system of white supremacy. Before morning classes, Meredith and his comrades would write signs on all the blackboards, which read, "MIAS vs. BIAS: who are you for?" Under cover of darkness, they delivered "subversive" anti-white supremacy literature to targets around Jackson. They dropped leaflets on the doorsteps of politicians, the chief of the Jackson police, even the Governor's Mansion. They never got caught.

By now, James Meredith was sharpening a political philosophy that was extremely radical yet rooted firmly in that most basic principle of American civics—citizenship. To Meredith, the usual discussion of civil rights and integration seemed timid and incremental. Such concepts were insults to the simple question of whether or not he was an American citizen. "To me, a person is no better off enjoying nine of ten rights than they are none of ten," Meredith explained years later. "My thing is the whole hog; either all of the citizenship rights, or none. I have no quarrel with the civil rights people," he explained. "It is just simply that their objectives are just so minute compared to mine." Paradoxically, the concept of integration was never Meredith's goal. His objective was the total destruction of white supremacy.

Meredith began developing an almost messianic vision of destroying the system of white supremacy in Mississippi, believing this was his "Divine Responsibility." Gradually, a bold strategic stroke Meredith had toyed with in the back of his mind was taking center stage: following through on his boyhood dream and registering as a student at the state-supported University of Mississippi at Oxford, where no Black students were ever known to attend.

Meredith chewed his idea over with his fellow activists at Jackson State, and one day he walked into the nearby office of Medgar Evers, introduced himself, and spilled out his thoughts. Evers, who in 1954 had unsuccessfully explored registering at the Ole Miss law school himself, had nothing but enthusiasm for Meredith's idea, and offered his support and the NAACP's legal resources when Meredith was ready.

The University of Mississippi was a multiracial, multiethnic institution that was open to almost every ethnic group on Earth. It hosted white, Hispanic, and Asian-American students, and welcomed nonwhite foreign-exchange students from countries such as Vietnam, Korea, Formosa (Taiwan), Pakistan, and India.

But the university had the absurd distinction of excluding just one group ever since it opened in 1848: The school refused to allow people of Black African descent to attend. The state university of Mississippi was closed to 43 percent of the state's own population, despite the fact that it was financed in part by hundreds of thousands of Black taxpayers. The majority of the members of the state's political structure and white population was dead set against letting Blacks in, and resolved to block with overwhelming physical force any Black who tried to enter the school. "Ole Miss," as the school was known (the nickname was used by antebellum slaves for the white mistress of the house), was located west of the city of Oxford in north-central Mississippi, a placid community perched on a ridge between the Yockony Patawfy and Tallahatchie rivers in the heart of the great Southern forest, on the very farthest western edge of the Appalachian foothills. It was a football-crazed institution, not an A-list school, but for generations of Mississippians, attendance was a crucial rite of cultural passage into the state's social and business elite. As Meredith observed, "It's better than Harvard at teaching you how to use 2 + 2 = 4 in Mississippi."

Lyceum, administration building at Ole Miss
(Photo courtesy of the Department of Archives and Special Collections, University of Mississippi)

Almost half the Ole Miss faculty held doctorates or other advanced degrees, far above the average for American colleges and universities. Despite poorly paid professors and regular assaults by segregationist state politicians on academic freedom of thought, Ole Miss students equaled or beat national norms in most fields in graduate exams, and the school produced more Rhodes scholars than almost every other Southern university.

The school occupied a gently rolling landscape west of the town square of Oxford. At the heart of the campus was the Greek Revival-style Lyceum building, where wounded Union soldiers from U. S. Grant's invading army were billeted in December 1862. "William Nichols patterned the Lyceum after an Ionic temple on the Illysis near Athens," wrote historian David Sansing. "The campus was in a setting of great natural beauty, with the buildings arranged in a semicircle at the crest of a slight eminence." The white-columned Lyceum was named after the Athens garden where Aristotle taught, and it housed the offices of the school's dean and registrar.

The idyllic splendor of the Ole Miss campus sometimes inspired outsiders to rhapsodic prose. "There are magnolias scattered among the elms, oaks, redbud and dogwood trees," wrote visiting Sports Illustrated writer Joe David Brown in 1960, "and on flat and sultry days their fragrance is everywhere, just as sentimental novelists claim. Mockingbirds sing in the trees, and on quiet nights when the moon is riding high katydids fill the air with a soft keening, and lightning bugs blink everywhere. In a state that celebrated the sport of football with sacramental intensity, the University of Mississippi was the holy shrine and tabernacle, home to some of the greatest playing in the country. "Inspired by Ole Miss, the whole state vibrates in a constant football flap," reported Time magazine in 1960. "Every

Ole Miss pep rally.
(Photo by Ed Meek courtesy Department of Archives and Special Collections, University of Mississippi)

Friday night the state is set aglow from the Gulf to the Tennessee border by the lights of high school games." The high priest of Ole Miss football was the legendary Coach Johnny Vaught, who lorded over the strongest coaching staff in the country and a squad of corn-fed homegrown players so massive that they looked as though they were wearing pads even when they weren't.

Visitors were often startled by the beauty of Ole Miss coeds, two of whom became consecutive Miss Americas in 1958 and

1959. Part of the charm of Mississippi women, wrote Joe David Brown, was "their dewy-eyed acceptance of their men as reckless and dashing creatures. If the women raise their voices at all, it is to squeal with delight or to feign terror at the accomplishments of the men."

(Photo by Kathleen W. Wickham)

East of the school, at the center of Oxford's Courthouse Square, was the white stucco Lafayette County courthouse, built in 1871, which was guarded by a thirty-foot-tall granite monument of a Confederate soldier gripping a long rifle. The statue was erected by the United Daughters of the Confederacy to honor Civil War veterans in 1907 and bore the inscription "They gave their lives in a just and holy cause." Union troops of General U. S. Grant's army invaded the square in December 1862 and stayed for only a few weeks, then returned in August 1864 on a rampage and burned down the old courthouse and much of the city. In 1962, the city was home to 4,700 whites and 1,300 Blacks who attended legally segregated schools and used segregated public facilities, as did all Mississippians.

On the north side of the Square was John Leslie's Walgreen drugstore, where you could park yourself on a stool at the fountain section and buy a hamburger for twenty cents, a J. Hungerford Smith-brand chocolate hot-fudge sundae for thirty-five cents, and a large Coca-Cola for a dime.

William Faulkner working at Rowan Oak, 1940
(Photo by Dan Brennan, Courtesy of Yoknapatawpha Press)

A few blocks south of the Square was the sprawling estate of Rowan Oak, the home of Oxford's most famous resident, Nobel Laureate and Pulitzer Prize-winner William Faulkner, arguably the greatest writer America had yet produced. He would sit on a beat-up chair by a sunny window, inhale the fragrance of gardens rich with magnolias and wisteria, and conjure up epic tales of murder and betrayal and doomed ancient destiny on his old Underwood portable, tales modeled on the real-life characters of Oxford and Lafayette County. "And he didn't exaggerate in those stories, he toned them down if anything," quipped his buddy, attorney Phil Stone. "That's just Mississippi."

In the April 1954 *Holiday* magazine, Faulkner sketched the baroque wilderness of his ancestors in an article titled "Mississippi." "In the beginning it was virgin," Faulkner wrote of his homeland, "to the west, along the Big River, the alluvial swamps threaded by black, almost motionless bayous and impenetrable with cane

46

and buck-vine and cypress and ash and oak and gum; to the east, the hardwood ridges and the prairies where the Appalachian Mountains died and buffalo grazed; to the south, the pine barrens and the moss-hung live oaks and the greater swamps, less of earth than water and lurking with alligators and water moccasins, where Louisiana in its time would begin."

Faulkner strolled the side streets of Oxford swinging his cane, and sometimes stopped to hover on the edge of the square. He would gaze at the courthouse, perhaps thinking up a new tale as he slowly packed his pipe with a rich tobacco blend lightened up with a pinch of Virginia bright. He always took his new manuscripts to Gathright-Reed's drugstore on the Square, where Mack Reed would drop what he was doing and hand-wrap the package for him for mailing to his New York publisher.

Some of the locals in Oxford were skeptical of Faulkner and thought he put on airs by dressing like a country squire, training horses on his front lawn, and generally acting aloof. An old friend once joked that Faulkner was about as popular as "a dead skunk in a sleeping bag."

At the university, where Faulkner once briefly served as postmaster before being fired for ignoring the mail in favor of scribbling out his stories, no Black person was ever known to have attended the school as a student. Black faces on campus were common, but only as maids, janitors, food-service workers, and workmen.

In fact, though, a light-skinned Black student from out of state named Harry Murphy, Jr., attended Ole Miss for nine months in 1945-1946 under the navy V-12 program without anyone realizing his race. He had several campus romances, ran track and field, and enjoyed punch and cake at church socials and square dances. He found it a charming place.

In 1950 a Black, artist named M. B. Mayfield became a janitor in the university's Fine Arts Center, and with the support of William Faulkner and Professor Stuart R. Purser,

Source Hottytoddy.com

the chairman of the art department, and his students, he sat in a broom closet during class and took notes as an unofficial student. He went on to become a renowned Mississippi artist.

In 1953 a Black minister from Gulfport, Mississippi, named Charles Dubra applied to the law school armed with a master's degree from Boston University and the backing of both the University of Mississippi chancellor and the law school dean, but Ole Miss trustees rejected him on the technicality that his undergraduate degree was from an unaccredited institution. Few other Blacks besides Medgar Evers had ever bothered to apply to the school, knowing they would automatically be rejected because of their race.

As he strategized with his allies, James Meredith could see some encouraging precedents for his idea of entering Ole Miss. Since the Brown decision in 1954, the public schools of Washington, D.C., Delaware, Maryland, West Virginia, Missouri, Oklahoma, Kentucky, and parts of Texas had begun desegregating. The state universities of Virginia, North Carolina, Georgia, Florida, Texas, Louisiana, Tennessee, Arkansas, Missouri, Oklahoma, and Kentucky had all accepted Black students or were in the process of doing so.

In February 1959 "massive resistance" to desegregation, a strategy articulated by a Democratic U.S. senator from Virginia, Harry Byrd, abruptly collapsed in his own state when fifty-three Black students were admitted to eleven all-white Virginia elementary schools. The theory of massive resistance called for overwhelming white opposition to desegregation and carried the implicit threat of riots or other violent opposition if integration was forced by federal authorities. But in Virginia, no blood was spilled.

In the "deepest" Southern states of Alabama, South Carolina, and Mississippi, however, Meredith could see discouraging signs. As noted earlier, in neighboring Alabama in 1956, Autherine Lucy had to withdraw from the state university hours after arriving, in the wake of white riots. The school remained closed to Blacks, as did the state university of South Carolina. Even those other Southern schools that were integrating were thus far accepting only token numbers of black students.

The most frightening precedents were in recent Mississippi history. In 1958 a Black man named Clennon King arrived in Oxford and announced his intention to register at the university. King was an eccentric, controversial minister and former instructor at all-Black Alcorn Agricultural and Mechanical College who triggered a student uproar and boycott in 1957 when he wrote a series of articles denouncing the NAACP and supporting segregation.

(Source: Mississippi Encyclopedia)

When he entered the Lyceum building, the Reverend King was escorted to an empty room and left alone for a while. University officials weren't sure what to do with him, since he refused to follow the normal process of filling out and mailing in forms and had brought some news reporters and photographers with him onto campus. Suddenly King began yelling for help, afraid his life was in danger. He shouted loudly enough for the reporters outside the building to hear, "They are going to kill me!" Mississippi governor James P. Coleman, who was monitoring the situation by phone, ordered state Highway Patrolmen to throw King off the campus. When King swore to keep coming back, Coleman ordered King packed off to the state mental institution, where he was imprisoned for twelve days. King soon fled the state.

In 1959 a decorated Black former U.S. Army paratrooper named Clyde Kennard tried to apply to all-white Mississippi Southern College. State officials charged him with allegedly helping steal twenty-five dollars' worth of chicken feed and packed him off to serve a wildly excessive seven-year term at the notoriously brutal Parchman Prison farm, where he developed stomach cancer.

But in 1960 James Meredith sensed reasons for hope and felt the time might soon be right for his own assault on Ole Miss. "Anybody who thinks all Blacks were on one side and all whites were on another has another thought coming," he recalled many years later. "There were plenty of people in Mississippi who wanted to see change. Mississippi was the most aristocratic state in America by far. Very few people controlled most everything major. These people were always generally opposed to the hard-core white supremacy. But nobody got out of line with the white supremacy ideology since twenty-five years after the Civil War."

During the fall 1960 presidential campaign, instructors at Jackson State College planned a student debate to mark the televised debates between Democratic candidate Senator John F. Kennedy and Republican candidate Vice President Richard M. Nixon. When no students were willing to argue for the Democrats, who for generations had stood for segregation and white control in Mississippi, Meredith volunteered. "You've got to understand," Meredith recalled in 2000, "[in Mississippi] all Blacks then were Republican. No one would take the Kennedy side of the debate. Consequently, I had to learn everything about the Kennedy campaign, which I did, almost word for word."

Meredith carefully scrutinized Kennedy's speeches as well as the strong Democratic party platform on civil rights, and when Kennedy narrowly won the election, Meredith decided the time was now right to put his plan into action.

One day after watching the flickering black-and-white TV images of John Kennedy taking the oath of office on January 20, 1961, James Meredith sat down at his Smith-Corona portable typewriter and wrote to the University of Mississippi, asked for a brochure and an application, and in so doing, quietly launched a one-man revolution. It wasn't the Olympian rhetoric of Kennedy's inaugural speech that inspired Meredith; Kennedy didn't even mention civil rights for Black Americans in his speech. "The objective," Meredith later explained, "was to put pressure on John Kennedy and the Kennedy administration to live up to the civil rights plank in the Democratic platform. It was an effort to force Kennedy's administration to either live up to it or suffer the public relations consequences of not doing what he was pledging."

"We are very pleased to know of your interest in becoming a member of our student body," read the letter from Ole Miss registrar Robert B. Ellis that came a week later. "If we can be of further help to you in making your enrollment plans, please let us know."

Meredith filled out the application and added a shocker of a footnote: "I sincerely hope that your attitude toward me as a potential member of your student body . . . will not change upon learning that I am not a white applicant. I am an American-Mississippi-Negro citizen." He concluded, "I certainly hope that this matter will be handled in a manner that will be complimentary to the University and the state of Mississippi."

Meredith explained he couldn't send the required five letters of recommendation from Ole Miss alumni in his home county, since they were all white and he didn't know any of them, so he enclosed recommendations of good character from five Black citizens.

By now, Meredith had accumulated a briefcase full of college credits and was three semesters away from a degree. In eight years of part-time study in the Air Force, he took dozens of college courses and passed them all, including tough courses in subjects such as the Russian language. As he was rotated to different postings, he studied at the University of Kansas, Washburn University, Wayne University, the University of Maryland, and the U.S. Armed Forces Institute. He earned the Good Conduct Medal and an honorable discharge. One thing was certain—if his ethnicity was anything other than African-American, James Meredith would have been welcomed to Ole Miss with open arms.

Meredith dropped his application in the mail. Within days, the University of Mississippi summarily cut him off.

On February 4 the Registrar sent a telegram: "It has been found necessary to discontinue consideration of all applications for admission" received after January 25. This was a brand-new technicality that was invented strictly to dispose of Meredith's application. The note said firmly, "We must advise you not to appear for registration."

Meredith expected this and quickly informed the Civil Rights Division of Bobby Kennedy's Justice Department in Washington, D.C., by letter: "It grieves me keenly to realize that an individual, especially an American, the citizen of a free democratic nation, has to clamor with such procedures in order to try to gain just a small amount of his civil and human rights."

Meredith also paid a courtesy call to the Federal Bureau of Investigation's resident field agent in Jackson. Meredith was well aware of the Mississippi government's practice of crushing dissidents, and he knew he might well need the might of the federal government to back him. He also knew he would need to draw national attention to his case, to avoid the underpublicized fates of people such as Clyde Ken- nard and Clennon King before him. "The objective," Meredith later explained, "was to make myself more valuable alive than dead."

At Medgar Evers's suggestion, Meredith had already written a letter on January 29 to NAACP counsel Thurgood Marshall in New York, asking for legal help from the group's famed Legal Defense Fund. "I am making this move," Meredith wrote Marshall, "in what I consider the interest of and for the benefit of: (1) my country, (2) my race, (3) my family, and (4) myself. I am familiar with the probable difficulties involved in such a move as I am undertaking and I am fully prepared to pursue it all the way to a degree from the University of Mississippi." But there was one problem: The esteemed Thurgood Marshall could not believe any Black person would be crazy enough to try to register at the University of Mississippi. The NAACP had no immediate plans for legal action on education in the state. Mississippi was so hopeless that it wasn't even on their target list. In fact, Evers had been exceeding his authority when he automatically promised legal resources to Meredith.

Marshall insisted on speaking to Meredith personally, to make sure he was sane and sincere. Meredith began speaking to Marshall on Medgar Evers's house phone, but grew furious at Marshall's incredulity—he thought his integrity was being questioned. Meredith cut off the discussion. He was going to move with or without Thurgood Marshall or the NAACP.

The journey might have died then and there. James Meredith had nearly infinite supplies of physical courage and mental determination for the struggle ahead and was very much the leader of this crusade in the making. But the NAACP had one thing he needed to succeed: a crack staff of battle-tested civil rights attorneys who could help him navigate the labyrinthine legal minefield that the state of Mississippi would force him into.

Medgar Evers stayed on the line, placated Thurgood Marshall, worked with Meredith, and kept the process going. Without Evers's intervention, Meredith's crusade would have ended.

At the NAACP Legal Defense Fund headquarters in New York, Thurgood Marshall walked into the office of Constance Baker Motley, a brilliant, methodical young associate counsel. Marshall dropped Meredith's letter on her desk, saying, "This guy's gotta be crazy!" Then he announced, "That's your case."

Motley asked, "Why me?"

(Source: Wikipedia.org)

Marshall joked that as a Black woman, Motley was less prone to physical attack in the Deep South than Black men, since many white men had Black "mammies," or nannies.

Meredith welcomed the involvement of Motley and her NAACP associate Jack Greenberg, a white attorney who successfully argued the Brown case before the U.S. Supreme Court. For his part, Greenberg thought that "Meredith was a man with a mission. He acted like he was an agent of God." According to Motley, "We never would have brought suit in Mississippi if it wasn't for James Meredith. Meredith had to have a Messiah complex to do what he did." Medgar Evers later observed of Meredith, "He's got more guts than any man I know, but he's the hardest-headed son-of-a-gun I ever met. The more you disagreed with him the more he became convinced that he—and he alone—was right."

James Meredith now harbored dreams of joining the business and political elite of Mississippi, and in the early days of his campaign to enter Ole Miss, he declared to a white reporter who visited him at Jackson State that he wanted to be governor. "James Meredith is crazy," concluded the reporter. "That's the best way to describe it. I think he's got a screw loose somewhere."

Actually, Meredith was simply a man who was ten, or twenty, or forty years ahead of his time, like a man from the twenty-first century dropped through a time warp into America's racial prehistory. The prospect of living out his life in the Dark Age of a segregated Mississippi was simply unacceptable to him. James Meredith wanted the world, and he wanted it now. As he later explained, "I asked myself the question, 'Why should it be someone else?' If people keep placing the responsibility with someone else, nothing will ever be accomplished."

In a letter dated May 25, 1961, the University of Mississippi unequivocally rejected Meredith's application for what it hoped would be the last time, expecting that Meredith would fold his cards, give up, and go away. The Registrar cited Meredith's lack of proper recommendation letters and, invoking a new technicality invented expressly to thwart Meredith, ruled that the school would not accept transfer students from institutions that, like Jackson State, were not accredited by the regional academic organization. "I see no need for mentioning any other deficiencies," Ellis declared. "Your application file had been closed."

Instead of walking away, Meredith packed his briefcase with color-coded files and on May 31, 1961, marched into the Meridian, Mississippi, courtroom of U.S. District Court Judge Sidney Mize, flanked by his lawyers and Medgar Evers and armed with a lawsuit.

Meredith's suit coincided with a fresh burst of civil rights action in the South in the first days of the new presidency. "The change of tide in Mississippi did not begin until 1961," wrote Mrs. Myrlie Evers. "Then, almost imperceptibly, Negroes took the offensive in the struggle for full citizenship." In March, nine students from Tougaloo Southern Christian College, a Black private school, launched a sit-in campaign at the whites-only Jackson Public Library. A new regional grass-roots coalition called the Student Nonviolent Coordinating Committee (SNCC) announced plans for a voter-registration project in Mississippi.

The most dramatic episode unfolded in May 1961, when the tiny Congress of Racial Equality sent biracial teams of volunteers into Alabama and Mississippi to conduct a nonviolent test of Supreme Court decisions banning segregation on interstate travel. On Sunday, May 14, a Trailways bus carrying the first team of Freedom Riders was captured by a mob of nearly two hundred white men outside Anniston, Alabama, who firebombed the bus and beat the volunteers until Alabama state policemen opened fire with warning shots.

An hour later, a second team of Freedom Riders was attacked in a Trailways bus at Anniston. When the bus escaped to Birmingham and pulled into the terminal, a frenzied mob of Ku Klux Klansmen ambushed and beat the Freedom Riders with lead pipes, injuring reporters and bystanders as well. The local police had helpfully allowed the Klan a fifteen-minute interval to attack and escape. When the rides resumed on Saturday, May 20, a mob of almost a thousand whites launched a riotous, savage attack on the Freedom Riders at the Greyhound terminal in Montgomery. The attacks triggered worldwide headlines and compelled federal authorities to protect the travelers with National Guardsmen. When the Freedom Riders made it to Jackson, Mississippi, they were peacefully escorted by city police and state Highway Patrolmen directly into jail.

Against this tumultuous backdrop, James Meredith appeared in U.S. District Court in Meridian, Mississippi on May 31, armed with a suit petitioning the court to direct his admission to Ole Miss, charging that the university refused his application because of racial bias. Judge Sidney Mize, distressed, as many other white Mississippians were, at the simultaneous arrival of the Freedom Riders to the state, summoned Meredith's attorney Constance Baker Motley back to his chamber and asked, "Why did you have to come now?" Motley replied that she couldn't pick her clients or their timing.

For the next sixteen months, Meredith and the NAACP lawyers dashed around the state, often tailed by Mississippi state government investigators, relentlessly pressing their legal fight while state officials fought back with an increasingly desperate campaign of evasion, delay, and obstruction. "I considered myself an active-duty soldier," recalled Meredith. "I was at war, and everything I did I considered an act of war." Meredith's spirits were buoyed by the fact that one of his lawyers was R. Jess Brown, one of only three Black attorneys in the state. "He was one of the men that I admired the most," remembered Meredith. "He was the only Black lawyer that would take those cases in Mississippi for many years. To me he was the important one."

Meredith's Byzantine legal struggle unfolded like a tale by Franz Kafka. On December 12,1961, District Judge Mize ruled, ridiculously, that Meredith was not denied admission on racial grounds. On January 12, 1962, the U.S. Fifth Circuit Court of Appeals in New Orleans ruled the university's policy of requiring referrals from alumni was unconstitutional. On February 3, Judge Mize reheard the case and ruled against Meredith, on the absurd grounds that the school was not a racially segregated institution. On June 6, Meredith was briefly jailed on a bogus false-voter-registration charge.

The case stopped and started over and over again, and sometimes Meredith, who continued his studies at Jackson State, feared he wouldn't succeed. For inspiration he read a quote from Theodore Roosevelt that he'd clipped out and carried around for nearly ten years. "It is not the critic who counts," the quote read. "The credit belongs to the man who is actually in the arena, whose face is marred by dust and sweat and blood . . . who at the best knows in the end the triumph of high achievement, and who at the worst, if he fails, at least fails while daring greatly, so that his place will never be with those cold and timid souls who know neither victory or defeat." He read the quote over and over, hundreds of times.

At last, on June 25, 1962, the U.S. Fifth Circuit Court of Appeals found that Meredith was rejected "solely because he was a Negro," and ordered Meredith's admission for the fall 1962 semester. "A full review of the record," wrote Judge John Minor Wisdom, "leads the Court inescapably to the conclusion that from the moment the defendants discovered that Meredith was a Negro they engaged in a carefully calculated campaign of delay, harassment, and masterly inactivity." In a peculiar backhanded compliment, Judge Wisdom noted admiringly that Meredith seemed "just about the type of Negro who might be expected to try to crack the racial barrier at the University of Mississippi: a man with a mission and with a nervous stomach."

Between July 28 and August 4, 1962, Judge Ben F. Cameron, a member of the Fifth Circuit Court of Appeals, issued four "stays," or delays, of the injunction. The first three were overturned by the full Court of Appeals, and Meredith and his lawyers appealed the fourth all the way to the Supreme Court. On August 31, the United States Justice Department entered the case for the first time as a "friend of the court," and petitioned the Supreme Court to rule for Meredith.

Finally, the case of Meredith v. Fair (referring to Charles Fair, chairman of the state Board of Trustees of Institutions of Higher Learning) was approaching the highest court in the land, but, with time running out and the fall semester already starting at Ole Miss, the Court was still out of session for the summer. Meredith's fate was now in the hands of Supreme Court Justice Hugo Black, the judge responsible for overseeing the Fifth Circuit Court of Appeals.

Justice Hugo Black was a native Alabamian who always carried a copy of the Constitution in his pocket. In 1923, when he was a prosperous trial lawyer, he joined the Robert E. Lee Ku Klux Klan No. 1 of Birmingham, and stayed active in it for two years. He later repudiated the Klan, but in an interview he gave to the New York Times on condition that it would be published only after his death, he explained that most Klansmen then "were the cream of Birmingham's middle-class. It was a fraternal organization, really. It wasn't anti-Catholic, anti-Jewish or anti-Negro."

Justice Black consulted all of his fellow Supreme Court justices by telephone, and on September 10, 1962, Black announced that each one agreed with him that he should issue an order to vacate all four of Judge Cameron's stays, enjoin Ole Miss from "taking any steps to prevent enforcement of the Court of Appeals mandate," and allow Meredith to register. In response three days later, District Judge Mize also ordered the university to immediately admit Meredith.

Now, after a stubborn, methodical, year-and-a-half-long legal campaign, James Meredith and his lawyers had finally compelled the University of Mississippi to admit him right away, on the same terms as white students. And suddenly, although probably nobody but Meredith realized it, the mystical young strategist had succeeded in forcing three new allies to his side: the president of the United States, the U.S. Justice Department, and the most powerful military machine in history.

In a matter of days, they, along with the rest of the country, would all be running to catch up with James Meredith.

William Doyle is the author of *An American Insurrection, PT 109*, and *The Sisterhood of the Enchanted Forest*. His book *Inside the Oval Office: The White House Tapes from FDR to Clinton* (1999) was a New York Times Notable Book. He won the Writers Guild of America Award for Best TV documentary for the A&E special "The Secret White House Tapes" which he co-wrote and co-produced. He is the co-author with James Meredith of *A Mission from God*.

NEVER!

By Curtis Wilkie

from *Dixie: A Personal Odyssey Through
Events That Shaped the Modern South,*
New York: Scribner, 2001
(used with permission)

Curtis Wilkie
(Source: Mississippi Encyclopedia)

On the last Saturday night of September, the football stadium at Jackson was filled beyond capacity. The regularly scheduled game between Ole Miss and the University of Kentucky had become a sideshow to the desegregation crisis, and the grandstand stirred with tens of thousands of Confederate battle flags. For years, the Ole Miss band had featured an enormous Confederate flag, so large that it covered most of the field, in halftime performances. But there had never before been many banners in the stands; flags blocked views and fans were discouraged from twirling them. But in the midst of the struggle with Washington, the flag had become de rigueur. The Stars and Bars flew on the radio antennas of cars and fluttered from windows of homes and office buildings across the state. The stadium was a red-and-blue sea.

In *The Past That Would Not Die* Walter Lord quoted a student describing the din: "It was like a big Nazi rally . . . It was just the way Nuremberg must have been."

That student was me.

At halftime, Governor Ross Barnett came onto the field, and the noise level reached a maniacal pitch as the crowd was informed of the lyrics for a new state anthem. The tune had been taken from Barnett's campaign song, "Roll With Ross," but fresh verses had been written and were flashed on the scoreboard:

> *States may sing their songs of praise,*
> *With waving flags and hip-hoo-rays;*
> *Let cymbals crash and let bells ring,*
> *Cause here's one song I'm proud to sing:*
> *Go, Mississippi, keep rolling along,*
> *Go, Mississippi, you cannot go wrong,*
> *Go, Mississippi, we're singing your song,*
> *M-I-S, S-I-S, S-I-P-P-I!*

As the thousands howled, Barnett lifted his arms in triumph. It was an incredible instant. Even as a dubious spectator, I could feel flesh crawling on my arms. I harbored strong misgivings about the governor; I thought he was an idiot. I did not wave a flag and I did not cheer. But I would not have traded my seat for a million dollars. I knew I was witnessing the final convulsions of the Civil War. All the crowd lacked were pitchforks and rifles. That would come the next night.

The interesting thing about Barnett at the Kentucky game the day before the riot, no one knew it, but Barnett had already basically sealed the deal with the Kennedys. He knew that Meredith was coming to the campus the next day, and nobody else did. There was an incredible mood of defiance in the air. For the first time, these small hand-held Confederate flags had been handed out to anybody who wanted them. They were handed out by the ASB, but probably paid for by the Citizens' Council or Sovereignty Commission. Barnett showed up for the game. It was not supposed to be part of the halftime performance, but the mood was such that he was thrust onto the field. They sang to the tune of Barnett's campaign song: "He's for segregation one hundred percent, he's not a moderate like some other gent. Roll with Ross, roll with Ross, he's his own boss." They encouraged everybody in the stadium to sing along with the "Roll Mississippi, we're rolling along" or something. I think the damn thing is still considered the state song, although nobody sings it today, thank God.

Barnett finally went out and said a few words, and in fairness to Barnett, he could have been much worse. He basically flapped his arms and talked about how he loved Mississippi, and he loved our people, and he loved our traditions and our heritage, and he kind of ended it at that, but it was quite a spectacle. It was pretty blood-curdling to me because I objected to so much of what was going on; and I remember there was an Ole Miss men's choir in back of Barnett—you can see it in some of the footage. Quite giddy, the crowd broke into song again, following words printed on leaflets passed through the stadium:

> *Never, never, never, never, No, never, never, never.*
> *We will not yield an inch of any field.*
> *Fix us another toddy, ain't yielding to nobody.*
> *Ross is standing like Gibraltar, he shall never falter.*
> *Ask us what we say, it's to hell with Bobby K.*
> *Never shall our emblem go*
> *From Colonel Rebel to Old Black Joe.*

Like most of my classmates, I woke the next day in Jackson a tad hungover, exhausted from the political passions of the previous evening, not knowing that Sunday's false peace would explode within hours. The first inkling of trouble came during the three-hour trip to Oxford. Driving back with my friend Franklin Holmes, we were passed by scores of speeding police cars. When we arrived on campus late in the afternoon, we saw the administration building, the Lyceum, surrounded by several hundred U.S. marshals, wearing white battle helmets and bulletproof vests. The protective gear looked incongruous over their dark business suits.

I'd like to think my journalistic instincts drew me into the crowd gathering on the grass circle in front of the Lyceum; perhaps it was a student's inquisitive nature. At any rate, I was about to get a lesson in mob psychology that had not been taught in the classroom.

Before sundown, the atmosphere had the feel of a pep rally; there were chants of the school cheer, "Hotty Toddy," punctuated by random rebel yells. But as the evening grew darker and more people arrived, the mood grew nasty. A federal force had been allowed to invade Ole Miss and capture the antebellum building that symbolized the school, and I detected both a growing sense of betrayal, directed for the first time at Barnett, and heightened rage at the Kennedys.

Students who had merely been heckling the marshals moved to more disruptive tactics. Though dozens of state troopers were on hand, the officers did little to discourage the taunting. I had the impression the state police felt they had been sold down the river by the governor, emasculated at a time when they had been spoiling to make a stand against the federal marshals.

A student flicked a burning cigarette on the canvas top of one of the military trucks that had conveyed the marshals to campus. When a marshal moved to extinguish the spark, he was pelted with eggs and debris. Another student produced a knife and began jabbing at a tire on one of the trucks. A state trooper helpfully pointed out an air valve as the most vulnerable spot. Rocks sailed and a couple of bottles broke into shards at the feet of the marshals. Still, the Mississippi troopers did nothing to restore order; some of them laughed at the marshals' discomfort.

Some protestors wore Confederate uniforms and waved rebel flags.
(Photo by Ed Meek courtesy Department of Archives and Special Collections, University of Mississippi)

From across the circle, I heard smashing sounds. A television cameraman had been attacked, his equipment flung away, and the windows of his car broken. The mob had grown fangs. I saw another photographer knocked to the ground. Someone snatched his camera, banging it against the pavement again and again. Blood gushed from a cut on the photographer's head. When a young faculty member attempted to stop the attack, I heard the sickening noise of fist striking skull, a sound I knew from roadhouse fights. The instructor fell, defended by no one. It was nightfall, and with a cover of darkness, more curses and rocks rained on the marshals. Suddenly, a noise of scattered poppings, muted explosions, broke over our heads followed by swirls of smoke. The marshals had fired tear gas into the crowd. Like schools of fish hundreds of students darted in different directions, shouting in panic. To escape, Franklin Holmes and I scampered across the Lyceum circle, now wreathed in noxious fumes.

The first campus riot in 1960s America was under way. Unlike the dozens to come later in the decade, ours was a right-wing uprising.

Fleeing, I got my first dose of tear gas. It scorched my face and burned my lungs. I could barely breathe. Coughing and crying, I found refuge in the lobby of a girls' dormitory, joining a group of stunned classmates. On a television set in the lobby, I saw the visage of President Kennedy delivering an address to the nation on the Ole Miss crisis. James Meredith was safely on campus, he announced. "This has been accomplished thus far without the use of National Guard or other troops." Invoking a theme he knew was dear to the South—its "honor and courage"—Kennedy talked of the valor "won on the field of battle and on the gridiron." He said there was no reason "why the books on this case cannot now be quickly and quietly closed," and he concluded with a message to the students of Ole Miss:

You have a new opportunity to show that you are men of patriotism and integrity, for the most effective means of upholding the law is not the state policemen or the marshals or the National Guard. It is you. It lies in your courage to accept those laws with which you disagree as well as those with which you agree. The honor of your university and state are in the balance. I am certain that the great majority of the students will uphold that honor.

The president did not know that, minutes before, all hell had already broken out on the Ole Miss campus.

Marshals are ordered to fire tear gas.
(Photo by Ed Meek courtesy Department of Archives and Special Collections, University of Mississippi)

Neither did the faithful at the First Baptist Church back home in Summit. At that hour, they turned their Sunday-evening service into a referendum on the Meredith situation. The congregation unanimously adopted a resolution:

Whereas, it is our firm conviction that the Word of God endorses the idea of segregation of races; Whereas, it is our firm conviction that integration of the school system in Mississippi would open an era of bloodshed, immorality, and crime unmatched in the history of our nation . . . Therefore, be it resolved that we stand solidly with our governor, Ross R. Barnett, in this solemn hour and pledge to him our loyalty throughout this great ordeal.

Instead of firing a few volleys of tear gas to disperse the crowd, the federal marshals, their patience exhausted, triggered hundreds of rounds. That stirred a wasp's nest. Rumors swept the campus, as insidious as the gas: a popular young woman had been struck and killed by a tear-gas canister; the grounds of Ole Miss were littered with many other student casualties; over the fallen Mississippi bodies, marshals were bringing Meredith to the Lyceum to be registered that night.

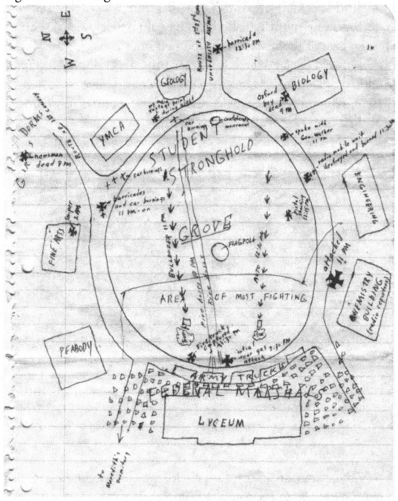

Curtis Wilkie sketch of the 1962 Ole Miss riot
(Image courtesy of Curtis Wilkie)

Eyes burning from the tear gas, students were stoked into venomous wrath by the various reports, especially by the word of the young woman's death. As soon as the first rounds of gas dissipated and Kennedy's brief speech ended, crowds surged back toward the Lyceum. The mob's numbers increased exponentially.

Within a half hour of the outbreak of fighting, the state troopers—who had maintained roadblocks at the gates of the school to keep troublemakers away—withdrew, leaving the campus open to posses of night riders. Cars filled with students from other schools in the state, eager to join the rebellion and unwilling to let Ole Miss enjoy all the glory of the insurrection, poured onto the campus. So did pickup trucks driven by seething men armed as if for a deer hunt. Hundreds of others flowed in on foot along University Avenue, carrying shotguns, sticks, rocks, and bottles. A construction project near the Lyceum provided a supply of bricks.

U.S. Marshals in front of Lyceum prepare to fire tear gas at the rioters.
(Photo by Ed Meek courtesy Department of Archives and Special Collections, University of Mississippi)

In the center of the Lyceum circle, the Confederate battle flag had been hoisted to the top of a flagpole.

By 9 p.m., control of the riot had passed from the students to the hands of an adult gang. From my vantage point at the foot of the circle, I watched as disorganized rioters made wave after wave of assaults on the Lyceum. I could hear ham radio units broadcasting appeals across north Mississippi for reinforcements.

Rioters commandeered the university fire truck, using the vehicle to charge the Lyceum. The scene looked like a distortion of a western movie: instead of Indians galloping around an embattled wagon train, the fire truck sped around the circle in front of the Lyceum like a toy out of control. Each time the truck passed the Lyceum, its passengers—clinging to the running boards—threw rocks and bricks and were met with broadsides of tear-gas canisters that struck the truck like heavy hail. After several circuits, the marshals captured the truck and its occupants.

Others picked up the fight. Uncoiling fire hoses, they sprayed the marshals' position with powerful jets of water. Although the mob was driven back again, the abandoned hoses continued to thrash and spew about the circle like giant, dying snakes.

Student demonstrators being held in the University of Mississippi Lyceum building.

(Photo by Ed Meek courtesy Department of Archives and Special Collections, University of Mississippi)

Rioters requisitioned a bulldozer from the construction site. A man who looked as though he had just come from a job clearing the backwoods fired the ignition and steered the grinding machine toward the marshals' redoubt. A cluster of insurrectionists marched behind him, pitching bricks into the blackness. They were met with fresh rounds of gas. The bulldozer barged into an oak.

The next assault was by car. Roaring across the grass circle, the driver collided with one tree and caromed into another, disabling the vehicle.

I thought it impossible, but the night grew more surrealistic.

Gangs uprooted concrete benches from the campus lawns and tumbled the debris onto the streets in an effort to block any convoys that might be coming to rescue the marshals. Inside the Lyceum, Robert Kennedy's press secretary, Ed Guthman, reported on the phone to his boss, "It's getting like the Alamo."

A layer of choking fog enveloped much of the campus. In my role as budding journalist and student voyeur, I wandered the fringes of the war zone, racing away when caught in pockets of gas and returning when it ebbed. I heard the rattle of gunshots and concluded that a firefight was taking place between the marshals and th

Burned vehicles lining the Circle after the rioting.
(Photo by Ed Meek courtesy Department of Archives and Special Collections, University of Mississippi)

Afterward, the federal government insisted that the marshals never resorted to firearms during the long night, a claim supported by a post-riot investigation. But if they had fired back, I would not have blamed them. Their situation, to use a newsman's cliché, was deteriorating rapidly. Through a veil of gas, I could see shadows, men crouching, firing pistols at the Lyceum. Marksmen with rifles climbed into trees to get better angles. Wounded members of the federal force fell at the foot of the building, exposed to further fire until they could be dragged inside by other marshals. Some in the mob dropped, too, struck by stray bullets.

Because no ambulances could fight their way onto campus, private cars were used to carry the wounded to the Oxford Hospital. I saw the mob block one car containing a bleeding marshal. The group finally allowed the vehicle to pass after determining the passenger might be dying. Such were the rules of war that night.

Nearly four hours after the riot began the first reserves came to the marshals' rescue. A convoy of Jeeps and trucks loaded with men in military gear tore out of the smoke along University Avenue and rounded the circle leading to the Lyceum. They were showered with bricks and bottles. A Jeep bounced off one of the concrete barricades, but kept moving. The next day we learned the members of the relief unit belonged to the Oxford National Guard; they were local merchants, insurance salesmen, and mechanics who had been put under federal orders to reinforce the marshals.

News of the coed's "death" proved to be untrue, but other reports were verified. The body of a foreign reporter had been found behind the campus YMCA. A spectator, Ray Gunter, 23, later identified as a "jukebox repairman" from Abbeville, was shot to death while watching events from the edge of the Grove.

When the melee began, several cars had been abandoned at the Lyceum circle. Thwarted in their attempts to storm the administration building, the mob directed its fury on the cars. They turned the vehicles upside down, then torched them. Flames licked from the windows, and burning wires caused the car horns to bleat mournfully.

Next, I feared, they would set fire to our buildings.

Ole Miss, a seat of Southern hospitality where the student motto had been Everybody Speaks, was being sacked by vandals from our own state.

I was not wise enough to perceive my own risk and stayed on the perimeter of the action for hours, enthralled by the bloody battle. During an interval in the fighting, Franklin Holmes and I spotted a face that had become familiar in the days leading to the riot. It was General Edwin Walker, standing near the Confederate monument, wearing a Texas cowboy hat and a dopey expression. In fact, he looked a bit dazed, as if he had swallowed a handful of tranquilizers. "Hell," I said to Franklin, "let's go talk to him."

We introduced ourselves to Walker and asked his assessment of the night. The general responded genially, saying the riot represented a great public outcry against the Kennedy administration. All the blood that would be spilled this night, Walker said, would be on the Kennedys' hands.

The old soldier asked us if the marshals were using bullets or buckshot to fight back. Since I was an ROTC washout, I knew little about weapons or military strategy and pleaded ignorance. "The marshals are clearly disorganized," the general offered, suggesting that they were probably running out of tear gas. If the mob wanted to overrun their position, he said, they should employ a flanking movement and attack from the south side of the Lyceum instead of constantly throwing themselves into a line of tear-gas fire at the front of the building.

Before the marshals could be overwhelmed, thousands of soldiers began arriving after midnight. Army trucks carrying troops in battle gear began lumbering onto the campus from different directions. They came down University Avenue and they came up Sorority Row, weathering barrages of rocks and bricks and Molotov cocktails. Bearing rifles with bayonets, helmeted soldiers swarmed through a western gate near a dormitory where Meredith had been sequestered throughout the night. Few of the rioters realized Meredith was there, or they might have redirected their attack from the Lyceum to his dormitory. Overhead we could hear the drone of a massive airlift, as troop transports descended, one after another, on the Oxford airport.

Franklin and I decided it was time to go back to the SAE house. Inside, there was bedlam. Many of our classmates were waiting to use the lone telephone to let their anxious parents know they were not among the casualties. In the distance, we could still hear the crump of tear gas, coupled with unearthly howling.

After dawn, platoons of paratroopers, working at bayonet point, finally drove the rioters off the campus. Skittering through side streets, the mob tried unsuccessfully to regroup in downtown Oxford. In the mopping-up operation, scores of men with no connection to the university were arrested. One of them was

General Walker.

By the time the battle was over, the campus reeked of tear gas. I expressed my dismay in a disconsolate letter I wrote home a few hours later, on Monday evening: "Dear Folks: It is rumored that we are now under martial law and that a 7 P.M. curfew is to be imposed." I gave a detailed ten-page account, written on lined notebook paper, of the riot the night before. I illustrated my story with a map showing the major points of conflict.

Thousands of troops were now on campus, I noted. "About a third of the campus population has evacuated. Others are leaving all the time. Classes have been forgotten. The semester is irreparably damaged."

I made my judgment: "No one is guiltless. Neither Barnett, the Kennedys, the Federal marshals, the Mississippi law officers, the NAACP, the Citizens Council. I hope they are happy because they have all contributed greatly to the ruin of our university . . . Right now it is impossible for me to attempt to salvage an education out of this mess. The mood is generally one of despair here. The campus is blockaded at all entrances as is downtown Oxford and all roads leading to the town."

After assuring my parents that I would not get involved in further trouble—I pledged to stay inside "because a gun battle between rednecks and troops might explode at any minute"—I added a postscript as though it were a news bulletin:

"I can hear tear gas bombs exploding across the campus. No one seems to know why . . . Jeeps incessantly patrolling the streets by the dozens. One tear gas bomb exploded in front of our house for no apparent reason. The troops are surely getting nervous. Planes, planes, planes overhead."

The final toll was two dead, countless wounded. Newspaper accounts simply said that "hundreds" were hurt. Various figures were published for the number of soldiers used to put down the riot, perhaps as many as thirty thousand. They never called it martial law, but Ole Miss lived under military occupation for my final semester. Despite my gloomy prediction, I completed my requirements and Meredith attended classes without further violence.

Curtis Wilkie served as Fellow of the Overby Center for Southern Journalism and Politics at the University of Mississippi. His books include *Dixie: A Personal Odyssey Through Events That Shaped the Modern South*, *The Fall of the House of Zeus: The Rise and Ruin of America's Most Powerful Trial Lawyer*, and *Assassins, Eccentrics, Politicians and Other Persons of Interest*. At the *Boston Globe* he served as a national and foreign correspondent and covered eight Presidential campaigns. He was the Globe's White House correspondent from 1977 to 1982 and served as its Washington bureau chief. He also was Middle East bureau chief for the Globe and covered such events as the 1982 Israeli invasion of Lebanon, the 1983 bombing of the U.S. Marines barracks in Beirut, and the first Gulf War.

A Student Editor Calls for Calm

By Sidna Brower Mitchell

(Photo courtesy of Sidna Brower Mitchell)

My father always told me, "You shouldn't judge people by where they live, where they go to church, how much money they have or the color of their skin. You accept people for who they are." My father's advice served me well in 1962 when I was editor of *The Daily Mississippian* in my senior year at Ole Miss and has been a central tenet throughout my life.

My thoughts as the incoming editor of *The Daily Mississippian* were how to get the newspaper in the black so the university didn't revert the paper back to a weekly. I rather doubt that I was deeply concerned about Ole Miss being integrated although the topic was certainly in the news at that time.

Sidna Brower at The Daily Mississippi, 1962,
(Photo courtesy of the Department of Archives and Special Collections, University of Mississippi)

As I started my senior year, girls still had to be back in their dorms or sorority houses by 11 p.m. so my days were spent going to class, focusing on the content of the newspaper and checking with university administration on the possibility of James Meredith entering the university. There were almost daily briefings with university officials after which George Street, Director of University Relations, would go to the steps of the Lyceum and relate Meredith's status to a handful of students and reporters. Little did any of us realize the violence that was about to unfold in just a few short weeks.

I recall a cameraman for a major network complaining he had fifty feet of film yet to shoot. He begged the gathered students to do something—even if only to dance! A male student obliged by climbing the flagpole in an attempt to put up a Confederate flag. That became the news of the day, and from then on I was cynical of the mainstream media.

Thankfully, I had two excellent managing editors—Jan Humber (Robertson) in the first semester and Ed Williams in the second semester so I could concentrate on my editorials and getting the newspaper out on time. I still contend that Ed, who retired as editorial page editor of *The Charlotte Observer*, is one of the best writers around.

On September 30, 1962, the media announced that a deal allowing Meredith to enroll in Ole Miss had been struck between Governor Ross Barnett and Attorney General Robert F. Kennedy, with Meredith being allowed to register for classes on October 1, 1962. I recall hearing the news after attending the Jackson football game and was eager to get back to campus as I knew I had to direct coverage of this event for *The Daily Mississippian*.

Upon my return, I found the Lyceum surrounded by federal marshals, elbow to elbow. The shameful and infamous Ole Miss riot had begun. People were hurling angry words, rocks and Molotov cocktails at the marshals. I barely missed being hit by a Molotov cocktail as I made my way across campus. How those marshals stood strong without retaliating as long as they did still amazes me.

U.S. Deputy Marshals guarding Lyceum building
(Photo by Ed Meek courtesy Department of Archives and Special Collections,
University of Mississippi)

I was meeting with other campus leaders on the second floor of the Student Union Building to discuss how to calm the situation when the marshals finally had to release tear gas. We had to leave quickly. I went to the journalism building to start working on a special issue of *The Daily Mississippian.*

The journalism department was in Brady Hall near the University Avenue entrance to the Ole Miss campus. Its central location made it a place where potential protesters stopped to ask directions. When an angry father with his son asked me where "the damn n----r" was, I realized we needed to lock the doors.

I told the local, state and national reporters and cameramen covering the riot that they could use the phones, typewriters and the darkroom in the journalism building. Later I was in the darkroom showing a photographer our process when there was a knock on the door telling us that Paul Guihard, a correspondent for Agence French Presse (AFP), had been shot. The photographer who was with me said, "Oh my God! That's my man!" and he immediately left.

We later learned that Guihard and a man from Abbeville, Ray Gunter, were killed and countless others were wounded. Jimmy Liddell, my advertising manager, and the Mississippian staff started a scholarship in memory of Guihard, but we never found out what the university did with the money.

Years later I learned that my cousin Dr. Gerald Hopkins was in the Lyceum treating whomever was injured—marshals, soldiers, protesters and others. He claimed the experience was horrific but also a physician's dream because he got to do his own triage.

U.S. Deputy Marshals guarding the Lyceum Building.
(Photo by Ed Meek courtesy Department of Archives and Special Collections, University of Mississippi)

During the riot, military vehicles and a car like mine were shown burning on television, causing anxiety for my parents. To no avail, they tried to call to make sure I was all right. Dr. Charles E. Noyes, the university provost, wrote to my parents, assuring them of my safety. Years later in a letter to me he said he was "praying to God, I had not given them false assurance."

After putting the special issue of *The Daily Mississippian* to bed, I was escorted through the Grove by a UPI photographer to the Kappa Kappa Gamma house where I lived. We had to dodge gun fire as we crossed through the trees. The next morning, I had to pass three checkpoints to get from the sorority house to the journalism department.

My circulation manager had refused to distribute the special edition, but Johnny Armstrong, a Phi Delta Theta, I had dated did. For years I thought he had Phi Delt pledges help disseminate the papers, but Johnny later revealed it was a reporter for *The Christian Science Monitor*.

The next day that same UPI photographer and I went out to Oxford Airport and watched as planes landed and unloaded Army troops. Along the runway were soldiers eight to ten deep. It was a frightening, yet humbling, experience. The National Guard had already been called out and reportedly 30,000 Army troops were deployed to Ole Miss.

One humorous moment happened when a soldier ran up to the officer showing us around to say that "the lady" has to get out of the area. It seemed the general or highest-ranking officer in a helicopter above us needed to use the latrine and I was in the way.

Starting with that special edition of *The Daily Mississippian* for which I wrote an editorial, "Violence Will Not Help," I wrote a series of critical editorials throughout the academic year that were related either to the insensitive actions of students or the lack of action by the university. As a result, I quickly became persona non grata among the student body. And, given the unfortunate national exposure Ole Miss was receiving at this time, I also found myself the subject of either criticism or praise in the local, state and national media. Note that the text of that first editorial which follows took no position on the integration issue,

Violence Will Not Help

Not only do the students chance forfeiting their education by participating in riots, but they bring dishonor and shame to the university and to the State of Mississippi.

When students hurl rocks, bottles and eggs, the Federal marshals are forced to resort to tear gas to back off the crowds.

When outsiders show their objections in the form of violence, they are seriously injuring the students in their attempt to continue their education. As a student, I beg you to return to your homes.

This is a battle between the State of Mississippi and the United States Government. The university is caught in the middle. The civil war was fought 100 years ago over almost the same issues and the United States of America prevailed. The Federal Government is once again showing its strength and power to uphold the laws of our country.

No matter your convictions you should follow the advice of Gov. Ross Barnett by not taking any action for violence. Blood has already been shed and will continue to flow unless people realize the seriousness of the situation. Whatever your beliefs, you are a citizen of the United States of America and of the State of Mississippi and should preserve peace and harmony.

Other editorials followed. In my "UM 'get tough policy' appears lost in crowd" editorial on October 31, 1962, I wrote "Why should students be suspended for yelling 'We want panties,' when they are allowed to throw rocks and yell profane and obscene comments at members of the United States Army" without fear of retribution?

On November 20, 1962, after seven students ate with James Meredith and had their rooms ransacked by other students, I wrote: ". . . if Ole Miss is to remain a true university and keep its scholars, all students should have the right to associate with whom they please and be able to say what they please without the fear of being chastised."

To some students, I had, in my editorials, "failed in time of grave crisis to represent and uphold the rights" of my fellow students. In fact, on December 4, 1962, the Campus Senate voted 63-27, to censure me. I found this to be the most hurtful experience of this difficult year. I quickly found out who were my friends and who were not, including the business manager of the Mississippian, whom I had appointed. I later learned that some folks voted because of their political ambitions. Unfortunately, this censure only caused more bad press in the national media for Ole Miss as the national media supported my editorial stance.

The faculty responded to the student censure by passing a resolution commending me for "unwavering determination to follow a constructive editorial policy." Further, they stated I had "significantly contributed to the preservation of the University's integrity."

The *Rebel Underground*, an underground student paper published on the Ole Miss campus during that time, frequently attacked both me and James Meredith. I was variously called "Sidner" or labeled as a "Pink Princess" and as "a disgrace to American journalism."

The Kappa Alpha fraternity started a petition to impeach me and went around to sorority and other fraternity houses to get signatures. They even came to the Kappa Kappa Gamma House. Although she was my good friend, Charlotte "Shotsie" Dreve as president quickly called a meeting in the living room. The girls took a vote and Shotsie went to the front door to tell Morris Spivey, the KA president, that the Kappas would not sign the petition. However, since two of my sorority sisters who lived at the top of the main stairs would often spit on me and call me names, they might have later signed the petition which fortunately did not go far.

Some of the coverage about me was so negative I became concerned that my editorials might affect my father's business, the majority of which was based in Mississippi. However, true to form, my father said, "Write what you feel is right." Years later I found a box of letters and notes from my father's customers, stating they agreed with me but were afraid to say that publicly because such statements might hurt their businesses.

While *The Jackson Daily News* was extremely critical of me in a front-page column by Jimmy Ward, some of the Mississippi weekly newspapers were supportive. Hazel Brandon Smith of Lexington and John Emmerich of McComb were two such editors.

Amazingly, the student body named me to the Ole Miss Hall of Fame in the spring of 1963 and that honor certainly restored some of my faith in my fellow students.

My editorials earned me numerous job offers, speaking invitations and awards, including being named one of 10 outstanding young women of the year in *Mademoiselle* and a nomination for a Pulitzer Prize. While I was greatly honored, I prayed that I would not win the Pulitzer. If I won such a distinguished prize as a 21-year-old college student how could I surpass it professionally?

Because I attended student conferences and made speaking engagements regarding the integration issues, I missed several classes. That was a problem for my achieving a minor in Spanish since the professor deducted two points off a final grade for every class missed. I changed my minor to history and told my Spanish professor. He walked over, briefly hugged me and said, "Bless you. I didn't want to fail you."

During a trip to Washington, D.C., to discuss an internship with Scripps-Howard, I was asked if there was anyone I would like to meet. I immediately answered, "Bobby Kennedy." That interview with the Attorney General was quickly arranged but I had trouble asking Robert F. Kennedy questions. He wanted to know about such issues as the feelings among the students, the probability of constructing housing for the Army troops that were camped on the football field, in the Grove and other sites on campus. When I returned to Ole Miss, I had a call from Washington suggesting I not write about my meeting with Kennedy because that could cause even more problems for me.

Thankfully, 40 years later the Associated Student Body repealed the censure and issued a commendation for "the outstanding journalistic courage she displayed throughout her tenure as editor of *The Daily Mississippian*." That was one of the most moving events in my life.

As I look back on my senior year, I am proud that I exercised the strength of my convictions regardless of the consequences and stayed true to the lessons my father taught me. I am grateful that I did have some supportive friends and professors, especially Dr. James Silver and his wife, Dutch, who worked in the office of the Dean of Women. She could sense when things were really difficult for me and would invite me to their home for dinner.

Dutch Silver would sometimes grant permission for me to stay out past curfew such as after the Peter, Paul and Mary concert. Law students Thad Cochran and Frank Hunger hosted a small party for the entertainers in their apartment. One person kept harassing Mary about personally inviting Meredith to the concert until Mary noted their bass player in the kitchen was a Negro. That guest then left, saying he felt compelled to alert students at the University of Alabama where the trio was to perform next. I quickly called and warned a close friend from high school, Jimmy Tackett, who was president of the student body there, about possible problems.

Dr. Silver, who befriended James Meredith, advised both of us never to meet or talk to one another. I didn't meet James Meredith until 40 years later at the open-door celebration, and then it was a chance encounter as we took the same shuttle bus from the hotel to the same location on campus.

Although I met fairly often with members of the university administration and federal officials such as Deputy Attorney

General Nicholas Katzenbach, Justice Department Attorney John Doar, who escorted Meredith on campus, and Chief Marshal James McShane, I was never told what I should or should not write in my editorials or in the news coverage. Years after moving to Bernardsville, New Jersey, I learned that Cyrus Vance, who had been Secretary of the Army in 1962, and Katzenbach lived nearby; however, I never had a chance to recall the days of the integration of Ole Miss with them.

Based on my father's influence and belief in accepting people for who they are and not on the color of their skin, I did not have a problem with the university being integrated. However, to express such an opinion, I felt, would only create more chaos and possibly severely hurt my father's business and any relationship with my mother's Mississippi relatives.

Writing this chapter on what happened at Ole Miss sixty years ago brought back tears and depression. But at least I didn't have the recurring nightmares that I had for almost five years after the riot. In those nightmares I could see the Molotov cocktails, the rocks and other debris hurled at the federal marshals and the National Guardsmen. I could almost feel the bottles splinter against the curb as I walked past the Lyceum. I could see and almost smell tear gas, hear the awful shouts and experience the hatred and confusion. I remembered people changing almost as fast as chameleons. Unfortunately, today I can see some of the same antics and hatred on television and in social media.

After graduating, Sidna Brower Mitchell had a Scripps-Howard Internship, working as a general reporter on the *World Telegram and Sun* in New York City and then as a deskman for UPI in London. Later, she as the director of employee communications for Citibank where she met her husband. Moving to New Jersey, the Mitchells purchased a weekly newspaper for which Sidna wrote a weekly cooking column for 42 years. She later joined the New Jersey Council on Affordable Housing (COAH), retiring as deputy director in 2002.

Paul Guihard: Murdered

By Kathleen W. Wickham

From *We Believed We Were Immortal: Twelve Reporters Who Covered the 1962 Integration Crisis at Ole Miss*. Oxford, MS: Yoknapatawpha Press, 2017.
(used with permission)

Kathleen Wickham at the Paul Guihard historical marker on the University of Mississippi campus.
(photo by Larry Wells)

Agence French-Presse reporter Paul Guihard was looking forward to enjoying his weekend in New York City when his editor sent him to cover the Mississippi integration crisis. Normally a copy editor, Guihard was given the assignment because the bureau was short-staffed. His editor, Jean Lagrance, recalled that Guihard was excited by the assignment because it took him away from the predictability of the copy desk.

Paul Guihard
(Photo courtesy of Alain Guihard)

He would return to New York in a coffin, the only reporter killed during the civil rights era. Lagrance would write in a memorial: "The offices of the AFP in the United States saw the brutal disappearance of one who they could count on in all circumstances. Paul was a friend to all. His sense of humor, his natural generosity, added to his professional qualities."

Though theories abound, Paul's murder remains a mystery. His case is listed by the FBI as unsolved, and unsolvable due to the passage of time. Evan Thomas, in his biography of Robert F. Kennedy, speculates that Guihard, seeing men unloading weapons near the Ward Dormitory, aimed his camera at them, and was shot in the back. Though Guihard was not a news photographer, his brother, Alain, of Lyon, France, said Paul habitually carried a small camera. A former Ole Miss coed at the scene partially corroborates Thomas's theory. She claims to have seen a man leaning over Guihard's body and smashing a camera into the ground. She, however, didn't witness the shooting.

Guihard's partial hearing loss in his left ear might also have been a factor. According to his brother, Alain, if danger came from his left side, he would have been slow to respond. Another theory involves an alleged dispute between a segregationist and another French reporter earlier in the day at the Robert E. Lee Hotel in Jackson. He was about Paul's height and had a red beard. This segregationist may have trailed Guihard to Oxford thinking he was the other reporter. An unidentified man dressed in white has also been named as a possible suspect. This possible assailant mentioned in FBI files was described as a sailor, or a kitchen worker. The Lafayette County sheriff blamed the killing on U.S. marshals. But no man, or group, has ever been positively identified as the killer. The fact that Guihard was shot in the back from a foot away meant the shooting was deliberate, not the result of random gunfire.

After arriving non campus Guihard moved without fear toward the chaos. As a young boy, living in St. Malo, France, under German occupation during World War II, he became adept at navigating

streets filled with enemy soldiers. Because of his dual citizenship, he served in the British army in Cyprus where he saw street fighting and learned how to take precautions.

Paul Guihard in the British Army
(Photo courtesy of Alain Guihard)

Guihard began his last day on a flight from New York to Jackson. Photographer Sammy Schulman, who worked for AFP as head of photo operations after a long and distinguished career with International News Service, accompanied him.

Schulman, 56, had photographed the 1938-1940 Finnish-Russian War, and then Sicily, Salerno, and French Morocco in World War II. He was the only news photographer present when President Franklin D. Roosevelt met with British Prime Minister Winston Churchill and French General Charles de Gaulle in Casablanca in 1943 under wartime secrecy.

The men complemented each other. Schulman was a scrappy New Yorker with a British wife. He could land in almost any city, in the midst of any crisis, and come out with the definitive news photograph. Guihard was a foreign newsman whose international view of events had been shaped by his youthful experiences living in St. Malo, France, during World War II. They were neither part of the story nor isolated from its greater implications.

As Guihard and Schulman boarded the plane in New York, Guihard shrugged off warnings from colleagues who had faced thuggish law enforcement officials in the South when Blacks demonstrated at lunch counters and bus stations. Guihard was blasé: "I'm going to pose as a Kentucky colonel and cover this thing with a mint julep in my hand."

During the flight to Jackson an airline stewardess, inquiring about his business in Mississippi, remarked, "Oh, I know, you're going down to the n----r thing." Guihard turned to Schulman and speaking French said: "These people. It'll take them a hundred years to start forgetting."

On arriving in Jackson, Guihard and Schulman rented a white Chevrolet and drove to the governor's mansion. More than 3,000 people had assembled at a rally sponsored by the White Citizens Council.

Two months after the 1954 *Brown v. Board of Education* ruling banning school segregation, the Citizens Council organization was founded in Indianola, Mississippi, in the heart of the Mississippi Delta. Chapters were formed across the South, and the organization was often viewed as an upper-class version of the Ku Klux Klan. Citizen Council members were typically drawn from community leaders, who used economic pressure, the media, and promotional materials to advocate their views. Gov. Barnett's political base could be found among the membership lists of the Citizens Council.

Mississippi Governor Ross Barnett (right).
*(Photo by Ed Meek courtesy Department of Archives and Special Collections,
University of Mississippi)*

At 11 a.m. that morning, Barnett released a statement to the press: "My friends, I repeat to the people of Mississippi now, I will never yield a single inch in my determination to win the fight we are engaged in. I call upon every Mississippian to keep his faith and his courage. We will never surrender." This message, broadcast over radio in the state capital of Jackson, attracted the attention of segregationists throughout the viewing area.

The governor's message was a call to action. Packing weapons and Confederate flags, rednecks, students from area colleges, and troublemakers from all over the South headed to Oxford. Their goal was to save Mississippi, to fight against change, and to preserve the citadel of learning known as "Ole Miss."

The scene was set for a violent confrontation.

Meanwhile, after the rally, Guihard walked into the Citizens Council's offices and interviewed Executive Director Louis Hollis. Guihard was a warm, friendly person and people were comfortable with him, sharing information and coffee. As a result he received permission to file his last story from Hollis' office. Hollis subsequently viewed Guihard as a friend, sympathetic to the council's opposition to Meredith's enrollment. Guihard's appearance in the council office took on new meaning after his death when segregationists claimed that Guihard was "one of them" and that a federal marshal had been responsible for his death. Neither claim was ever substantiated. Guihard was just a reporter looking for a phone.

Then, it was late afternoon and time to head to Oxford, a trip that would take almost four hours. As Guihard and Schulman drove north, they listened to President John F. Kennedy's 8 p.m. speech on the radio. The broadcast included the news that Meredith had arrived in Oxford and that the atmosphere on campus was calm. Unbeknownst to Kennedy, moments before he went on the air the order to fire tear gas had been given, setting off a full-scale riot. Kennedy, in his prepared speech, reminded listeners: "In a government of laws and not of men, no man, however prominent or powerful—and no mob, however unruly or boisterous—is entitled to defy a court of law."

"Oh hell, the story's over," Guihard said to Schulman in the car. "But we might as well go and clean it up." A Mississippi Highway patrolman stopped Guihard's car as it approached the campus at around 8:40 p.m. The officer warned the pair, "I can't guarantee your life or property if you drive in." Guihard acknowledged the officer's warning and drove onto the campus toward the Confederate statue dedicated to university students who fought in the Civil War. There were no barriers, and people were coming and going.

The pair parked and walked toward the crowd of angry students and outsiders. Night had fallen. The grounds were dark and the stench of tear gas was in the air. The roar of the mob rolled across campus.

As Guihard and Schulman moved through the campus, they encountered dark figures darting back and forth. Photographers were advising each other to "shoot and run." The flash bulbs gave them away, and the mob attacked them and smashed their cameras.

Guihard and Schulman decided to split up. It was both a newsman's tactic and a military maneuver. They had different but complementary duties that night and by splitting up more ground could be covered. At the same time a reporter doesn't necessarily walk straight into chaos but flanks the scene and observes without barreling through the crowd. Guihard told Schulman, "I'll see what's doing and see you back here at the car in an hour, then."

Less than ten minutes later he was shot in the back from one foot away, the bullet tearing into his heart. His body was found by students in a dark area of campus near a women's dormitory. The location was out of sight of the federal officials protecting the campus.

An experienced reporter like Guihard knew the risks involved in street reporting. Tensions are often high. Protagonists face off against antagonists. But he didn't say, "I can't go there, that's too dangerous." It was his job to get the story. As a journalist he was committed the moment he accepted the assignment. It's almost like taking holy orders. He doubtless thought to himself, "I'm going to go forward even if it is a mob." He could seek a safer path by circling the action, taking shelter if gunfire erupted, but he could not cover the riot from inside a newsroom. He could keep an eye out for fellow reporters stationed in the Circle, the 3.5-acre green space in front of the Lyceum where the riot was underway, and from them learn what was happening. Various people said they thought they saw Guihard in the tear gas smog, or perhaps spoke to him as he ambled across the greenspace. But then he disappeared in the miasma.

It is said that some people are born to be musicians, writers, or artists—that creative souls are born, not made, and that youthful interests do not translate into a career without the influence of others. Paul's influences were war-torn France, where print and radio news was censored and propaganda was the norm.

His parents sent Paul and his brother, Alain, to live with their grandparents in St. Malo, France, during the early days of the London Blitz. Their mother Betty Crowther, who was born in Yorkshire, met his French-born father while working at a hotel in the Guernsey Islands. They spent the war years managing the hotel they owned in London. Alain was just an infant at the time and Paul was seven years older. They would not see their parents again until the war ended in 1945.

Paul and younger brother Alain.
(Photo courtesy of Alain Guihard)

For the young boys, life on the Brittany coast was a lonely, wistful existence marked by shortages of food, clothing and school supplies. Their clothes became tattered rags yet were worn until they were long outgrown. The boys and their grandparents were evacuated inland when, after D-Day, the Allied bombs rained down, destroying most of St. Malo.

St. Malo fortress ramparts
(Photo by Kathleen W. Wickham)

Their beach playground, the Plage de Bon Secours, with its saltwater pool became a minefield, while the medieval walled citadel with its labyrinthine network of cobbled streets and ramparts sheltering massive granite buildings was almost totally destroyed. The steeple on the Roman Catholic Cathedral of St. Vincent suffered the indignity of collapsing inside the structure under the Allied shelling. Adventure surrounded the boys too, in the history of St. Malo. In the 17th and 18th centuries France granted St. Malo's sailor merchants, known as corsairs, license to act as pirates, "coursing" after enemy ships and earning a portion of the proceed.

Alain Guihard said his brother Paul "couldn't resist reading a newspaper from beginning to end," as if he had to consume all the day's news in one sitting. It is easy to see how from the ramparts of the walled medieval old city fronting the beach a boy missing his parents could imagine he could see England across the channel, and with the information pulled from a newspaper, living in an occupied country and knowing of the history of St. Malo would want to explore the world through the power of journalism.

Alain Guihard, 2016, St. Malo, France
Photo by Marie Gerard

It was this quest for knowledge, the curiosity to know the truth and the desire to create understanding that propelled Paul into the morass.

Guihard became a full-time AFP staffer in 1953 after returning from the British military service. He spent a year in Paris at its English-speaking news desk before he was transferred to New York in 1960. He covered a variety of assignments including a flood disaster in Honduras and the Cuban missile crisis. While in New York he also freelanced for the *Daily Sketch* of London. At the time of her son's death, his mother observed that Paul had "wanted to be in newspapers since boyhood. He never wanted to do anything else."

To the Rev. Michel Leutellier, who grew up with Guihard in St. Malo, it was no surprise Paul became a writer and journalist. Leutellier recalled that Paul could be found at lunch writing in his tablet. Though some of his teachers disapproved of his satirical writings, he edited a school journal called *The Lame Duck*. He produced two editions of about thirty pages each, with contributions from about ten other students. "When he wrote, it was pure French and very pleasant. He had a lot of ideas and he knew how to present his ideas in a very original way."

Leutellier recalled, "We were boys together and then young men. We discussed different things from boyish matters. We talked about philosophy, history, politics, etc. He was very interesting for me because in the seminary and even at school [we had not] this widening of the mind he could have [learned] in a journalism school."

Leutellier, who went on to become a parish priest, said he kept in contact with Guihard over the years and followed his journalism career from afar, observing he was always taking risks in his work. "I was doing my military service, and I was going to Senegal; so I got in touch with Paul before leaving. He saw me in uniform, and when leaving the house, he said, 'If you were in the British army, we would give you two weeks in the military jail. You're all buttoned down, but your shoes are not shiny.' I remember we laughed, but I think the British army was not very kind with its soldiers."

According to Leutellier, Paul was a loner who walked home for lunch to his grandparents' home in St. Servan, a suburb of St. Malo. He was one of the "privileged" class of students whose family could afford tuition. His clothes, purchased in England had a different cut and style than those worn by his schoolmates. "In those days, that was a big difference," Leutellier said.

Today, Paul's elementary school run by the Christian Brothers is little changed. Classrooms surround a playground where Leutellier recalled spending recess with Paul during the German occupation. It takes only a little imagination to think of the games Paul played while working on his satirical cartoons and stories—the defeat of the Nazis, France's victory over tyranny, life in London with his parents, the future.

At 17, he covered the 1948 London Olympic Games for Agence France-Presse. Nearly fourteen years later his life ended at the University of Mississippi. *Life* magazine photographer Flip Schulke, who may have been the last newsman to speak to him, watched Guihard heading up a street toward the Lyceum. "I yelled, you know, *get down!* And this French accent came back at me, saying, 'I'm not worried, I was in Cyprus.'"

As Schulke huddled under the shrubbery, Guihard disappeared into the tear gas behind the Fine Arts building. *New York Herald-Tribune* reporter Robert S. Bird's description of covering the riot provides a playbook for how Guihard probably faced the danger that led to his death. Bird wrote:

> *A reporter doesn't exactly cover a riot of that kind in the conventional sense—with pen and pad in hand, I mean. You uncap your ballpoint and hold it in your trouser pocket to jab into the eye of the first maniac who tries to slug you. You slip your notepaper into a rear pocket in case you need it to wipe the blood away.*
> *You don't rush into a riot. You sidle up to it warily and allow yourself to be sucked into it. For it is already out of control and has its own brainless system of dynamics. You understand full well that you personally, as a news reporter, are a prime target for the mob if your identity is discovered. You're scared to death, but there's no time to think about that. Suddenly you are right in the middle of it all and you must now deal with the immediate action swirling in a 20-foot radius.*

Into that swirl Guihard vanished.

Unlike other members of the press corps, who had arrived on campus days before and were issued press passes, Guihard, due to his late arrival, carried no such identification. He also was unknown to the press corps. What made him stand out were his stature, his red beard and his accent. Schulke said, "I always remembered [Guihard's statement] because I didn't know much about Cyprus, but [Ole Miss] was a dangerous place."

Schulke, underscoring Bird's observations about how a journalist proceeds into a riot, but speaking as a photographer, said, "The camera is like a wall between you and danger, and you take chances. I had never been under fire before. You wonder if it's worth it . . . I reached a point where I decided that if I was going to risk my life, it had to be for something I truly, deeply believed in."

Gunshots rang out repeatedly that night. Another man, Ray Gunter, was killed standing near the Hilgard railroad bridge at the university's main entrance. Gunter was from Abbeville, a dozen or so miles north of Oxford. A jukebox repairman, he came to see what all the fuss was about. His first child was born the next day. His assailant also was never identified.

The U.S. marshals were told to not fire their weapons and did not, except in rare instances. For Robert Kennedy, who as attorney general was charged with seeing that federal laws were enforced, the decision not to return fire was painful. As Evan Thomas wrote: "Say no to defensive fire and [Kennedy] risked sacrificing his men, several of them dear friends, and letting the mob string up Meredith from one of the gracious oaks in the Grove. Say yes and he risked provoking a second Civil War."

Tear gas explosions in the Circle
(Photo by Ed Meek courtesy Department of Archives and Special Collections, University of Mississippi)

As Guihard headed toward the Circle, the mob surged in his direction. Schulman veered in another direction, skirting the 10-acre Grove, a hallowed ground presently used for tailgating before football games. A student told him to hide his cameras as "some bums up there (near the Lyceum) are smashing them."

It is not known if Guihard ever made it as far as the Circle. His body was found at the southeast corner of the Ward Dormitory, about 12 feet east of the building's wall and about 55 yards from Grove Loop Street, also east of the dormitory.

To Meredith, an Air Force veteran, Guihard was simply a casualty of an armed conflict. When asked for his reaction to Guihard's death he remained noncommittal: "What soldiers do is kill enemies. If there was any real surprise to me, it was that only two people got killed."

Students walking in the area near the Fine Arts building found his body around 9 p.m. Education major Hugh Calvin Murray of Meadville, Mississippi, told FBI investigators a female student stopped him while he was walking in front of Ward. She said, "Oh look!" and pointed toward the east end of the building. Murray said he observed "a man lying on his back with his feet extended out onto the sidewalk." The site was near a clump of bushes in an unlit area.

Johann W. Rush, a freelance photographer from Jackson working as a stringer for CBS, said some thought that tear gas had felled Guihard. Murray "advised that he assumed that this person had suffered a heart attack. He immediately removed the glasses from this person and began massaging his heart. He recalled that the victim had a slight pulse beat; however, he did not feel a heartbeat. He estimated that he massaged this person's heart for at least 30 minutes when another person came by, believed to be a student, name unknown, who relieved him, and this person massaged his heart for another 20-30 minutes."

Pharmacy student Tom Brown of Jackson, Mississippi, said when he arrived about a half dozen students were already present, and they had elevated Guihard's feet believing him to be in shock. "I asked if he had any pulse. They said he did. I checked and found no pulse. There was no air escaping through his nostrils or his mouth and his eyes were thoroughly dilated. There was no heartbeat to my knowledge. I put my ear to his chest and could not hear a heartbeat. However, we continued to massage his chest, and we once tried mouth-to-mouth resuscitation. But to no avail. I am sure and was sure at that time that the man was dead," he recalled.

During the time Murray was with Guihard, the victim uttered no sound. Murray estimated that no more than ten individuals came by the area. He recalled that someone, possibly one of the housemothers from a nearby girls' dormitory, brought a blanket and covered Guihard's body.

Murray told the FBI that he was not aware that the man had been shot and could not recall seeing any blood on his brown coat. Brown, however, noted that Guihard had bitten his lip and there was dried blood on his lip.

Cort Best, a photojournalist with the Courier-Journal and Louisville Times in Kentucky, said that, although he was at the scene shortly after the students discovered Guihard's body, he did not take photographs at the request of a housemother at the scene.

Meanwhile, other people were working on getting help for Guihard. R.J. Bonds, a radio station manager in nearby Batesville, told FBI investigators that he was in the YMCA building near the Confederate statue when a person he assumed was a student came in and asked to use a telephone to call an ambulance. The ambulance, however, could not get through the crowd. Help came from the campus infirmary in the form of a student with a car.

Rush and Brown said they and several other students used the blanket to carry Guihard to the car to take him to the city hospital on Van Buren Avenue. They had to carry him through the Ward dormitory as the car was parked in the rear. Brown said the student with the car arrived about 10 or 15 minutes after he arrived: "A boy rode up in a car—or he walked up, his car was behind the dormitory and said we could put the man in his car and he would take him to the city hospital in Oxford."

Graduate student Donald Lee Dugger of Independence, Missouri, said he was one of the three people who that transported Guihard to the hospital. Dugger told the FBI he went to the student infirmary to assist his wife who worked there and was asked to "remove Paul Guihard from Ward Hall to the Oxford Hospital."

Brown recalled that, 10 minutes later, an ambulance arrived and he informed the driver that Guihard had already been transported to the hospital.

Murray Sutherland, an ambulance driver for the Douglas Funeral Home, said that he drove to the hospital to determine the man's status after learning Guihard's body had been taken to the hospital: "We learned that he was DOA, that he was a citizen of France, and they would have an inquest."

Mayor Richard Elliott, who owned a funeral home, said he initially learned of Guihard's death when a student stopped him on the Square saying that someone had had a heart attack on campus and a doctor and ambulance were needed. Guihard's body was taken to Memphis for autopsy. It was there it was noted that a bullet had penetrated the back from a foot away.

Schulman learned of Guihard's death while examining the equipment in the photo lab of the student newspaper, *The Mississippian*. Editor Sidna Brower said she was showing Schulman the lab when someone knocked on the door and informed them of Guihard's death. "Oh, my God, that's my guy," Schulman cried. Brower does not recall the time, only that the newspaper had made its darkroom, newsroom and telephones available to the visiting media. The student newspaper was in Brady Hall, near the University Avenue entrance to campus, about a quarter-mile from the Lyceum.

Schulman formally identified Guihard at the funeral home and picked up Guihard's personal effects at the hospital, signing a receipt. Hospital records indicated Guihard was already dead from a gunshot wound when he arrived at the hospital.

The first news report of Guihard's death was stated in a one-sentence telegram sent at 10:59 p.m. to *The News and Courier*, Charleston, S.C., by Anthony Harrigan. Ten minutes later, at 11:09 p.m., Richard Starnes, a reporter for the Scripps-Howard Newspaper Alliance, had Western Union transmit a complete story about the night's events with a paragraph about Guihard's death below the lead.

The White House learned of Guihard's death at 12:30 a.m., October 1, when Jack Rosenthal, a special assistant to the attorney general, called the White House seeking to speak to Assistant Attorney General Burke Marshall or Robert Kennedy. The president's secretary, Evelyn Lincoln, who answered the call, took the message from Rosenthal: "Would you tell him that a reporter for the London *Daily Sketch*, whose name is Paul Guihard, was killed in Oxford just now? His body was found with a bullet in the back, next to a women's dormitory." (Guihard occasionally wrote for the *Sketch* but was on assignment for AFP)

The president sent a telegram expressing his condolences to Jean Marin, president and director general of Agence France-Presse in Paris:

I want to express to you the shock of the American people on the death of your correspondent, Paul Guihard, last night in Oxford, Mississippi. The American people, I am sure, as well as the law-abiding citizens of the state of Mississippi, share my sorrow that this could have happened in our country. I hope you will convey my condolences to his family.

President Kennedy arranged to have an Air Force C-47 plane transport Guihard's body to New York for a memorial service. The service was held October 5 at the French Roman Catholic Church of St. Vincent de Paul on 23rd Street near Sixth Avenue. AFP made the arrangements to fly Guihard's remains to France via Air France. No family members were on the flight, but Alain Guihard met the plane when it landed at Orly Airport in Paris.

Flowers were placed on the spot where Guihard died the next day. Paul Mathias, the American correspondent for Paris Match, a French news magazine, conducted his own investigation and came up with no suspects.

Alain Guihard had last seen his brother three years before his death. While completing his military obligation in Algiers, Alain would receive long letters from Paul concerning his ambitions to be a playwright and life in New York. He was still in Algiers when he heard a radio announcement of his brother's death: "His name was given, no possible doubt." Alain was scheduled for discharge within the week and the British Army arranged for him to leave immediately. Alain met Paul's plane drove to St. Malo.

Their parents learned of Paul's death from AFP's London manager. Alain recalled: "You can imagine the shock to them, but my mother, more than my father, managed to control her emotion, and went on carrying out her usual tasks, without anyone noticing the difference, so she said!"

The death of Guihard stunned his colleagues. Jean Lagrange, U.S. bureau chief for Agence French Presse, wrote a memorial letter published in *The Washington Post*:

Paul Guihard died in the achievement of his journalistic mission such as he conceived it: on the same ground of the action. He knew the risks that are of the first lines. But he accepted them with a calm courage and with a profound sense of responsibilities;

he did not want to describe what he had not visually witnessed, with objectivity and sincerity. Saturday evening, I spoke to him to develop this report, which was to be, for him, the last.

As always, he was delighted to drop his usually work routine of writing, with his usual enthusiasm, toward a new professional experience. His name lengthens the too-long list of those who, in their profession, have, like him, been victims of their desire to serve the cause of honest information.

The Agence French-Presse lost a talented colleague. The offices of the AFP in the United States saw the brutal disappearance of one whom they could count on in all circumstances. Paul was a friend to all. His sense of humor, his natural generosity, added to his professional qualities, we will miss now.

Paul Guihard
(Photo courtesy of Alain Guihard)

In their eulogies, colleagues recalled Guihard's nickname of "Flash," earned because of his passion for journalism. Friends also described the bearded, husky, six-foot tall bachelor as a "bon vivant." Felix Bolo, an AFP editor on duty the day Guihard was killed, wrote in a letter to historian William Doyle, "He had a great sense of humor, English or French, and he always seemed to be happy, kidding and joking all the time. He was a 'force de la nature,' as we say in French. He would have made an excellent movie actor, a natural and huge Rob Roy."

Paul Guihard is buried in the family tomb in St. Malo. AFP sent a representative to the funeral. Leutellier conducted a traditional Catholic burial service. Paul Guihard's family accepted the inevitable and moved on. According to Alain: "My mother dealt with it in the best possible way on the day they learned about it. She went on with her usual work in the hotel. My father took it more dramatically. I think really for both of them it's that sort of event, which stays with you throughout your life. One of the worst things, I think, for parents, is to lose a child. There's nothing worse."

Dr. Kathleen W. Wickham is a professor in the School of Journalism & New Media at the University of Mississippi. She is the author of *We Believed We Were Immortal: Twelve Reporters Who Covered the 1962 Integration Crisis at Ole Miss.* A memorial bench on campus honoring Paul Guihard and a plaque designating the UM campus as a national historical place in journalism recognizing the 300+ reporters who covered the integration crisis were made possible through grants provided by the Society of Professional Journalists when she was chapter advisor.

Safeguarding James Meredith

By Henry T. Gallagher

From *James Meredith and the Ole Miss Riot: A Soldier's Story*.
Jackson, MS: University Press of Mississippi, 2012.
(reprinted with permission)

(Photo courtesy of Henry Gallagher)

At 0500 hours, on October 1, 1962, the 716th Military Police Battalion from Fort Dix, New Jersey (less than full-strength since the "step-back" of the Black soldiers), with 140 assorted vehicles, including an ambulance and a mess truck pulling a water trailer, rumbles through an Oxford citizen's side driveway and out the other end. One can only wonder how long it took for the convoy to clear her property.

We've arrived. An Army of the North. A bit less dramatic than Sherman's arrival in the South almost one hundred years earlier. Yet in some quarters down here (and surely in that woman's house back there), we are just as unwelcome now as the Yankee was then.

The convoy pulls up along a tree-lined residential street just short of a big intersection. I sense that we're on the edge of the university. Across the street I see a lane that I guess runs up onto the campus and to the noise and the tear gas and the reason why we're all here this morning. By now the sun is about three fingers above a stand of trees off to my left. I don't know much else at this moment, but I know which direction is east.

Lt. Henry T. Gallagher, 1962
(Photo courtesy of Henry Gallagher)

I can see better now. And can reflect for a moment, and only a moment. I could do little of that when we got lost back there. Must be just a few blocks over from here. At the time I felt a charge of excitement—but the fear kind. Bricks, concrete chunks, whatever could be thrown were. And then a rush of adrenaline followed. It was the kind that soldiers will feel five years later in Vietnam, only, for them, a rush jacked up by a multiple of fifty or more. Mine was a minor one, but a rush of something. Whatever. (That's a Minnesota word that one says for a lot of things, like when you don't know what else to say—you say "whatever.") When I saw two of them ready to throw concrete chunks at us, but a few feet away, it was a quick down-up sensation that came on—first, fear, and then, well, that rush of whatever—not unlike that first fight you had in the alley as a kid.

The challenge awaiting MP Lt. Henry Gallagher—an effigy of
James Meredith displayed outside an Ole Miss dormitory.
(Photo by Ed Meek courtesy Department of Archives and Special Collections,
University of Mississippi)

Lieutenant Pete Frechette brings his platoon up in jeeps. His
NCOs check out the men. Rifles at the ready, bayonets fixed and
unsheathed, gas masks on. His small group passes us, crosses the
intersection, and rolls up the lane in the direction of the campus. In
so doing, the 716th (Task Force Charlie) has entered the fray. The
platoon, as regular army MPs, has trained for such emergencies,
yes. But, except for my bare-bones radio message and quick jeep-
side briefing to the colonel and Lt. Frechette, it lacks both practice
in dealing with and knowledge about what it will confront at the
end of the lane.

Later I find out that the MPs in the 503rd (Task Force Alpha)
and the soldiers in the 2nd Division (Task Force Bravo) knew their
missions ahead of time.

Once the platoon reaches the campus and finds the Lyceum, Lt. Frechette is led over to a general officer who's seated in a folding chair at a card table. It's Brigadier General Charles Billingslea, commander of the 2nd Infantry Division at Fort Benning, the same one-star officer to whom I had reported at the airport earlier this morning. The top army officer in the operation in a folding chair! Field expediency. Must've been the one he had back in the van at the airport.

The general orders Frechette to have his men clear the area near the Lyceum of any remaining rioters that may still be on the campus and to move to the downtown section of Oxford.

U.S. Army troops clear campus of rioters
(Photo by Ed Meek courtesy Department of Archives and Special Collections, University of Mississippi)

At 6:00 with a light drizzle chilling the air, a mob of young toughs had gathered on the corners of Lamar Street and University Avenue, near the town square, pitching Coke bottles at jeeploads of soldiers hurrying by. A few yards away, a group of state police leaned languidly against their cars and watched.

Unlike me, who hesitated to ask questions, Frechette has the good sense to seek further advice from this general. He turns back to ask the one critical question that's on the minds of everyone sitting out in their waiting jeeps in front of the Lyceum.

"Yes, sir, but now, sir . . . just where is this downtown?"

He gets back into the lead jeep and heads down University

Avenue toward the square.

Three carloads of troopers sat passive in a filling station while a mob threw rocks and bottles at passing army trucks. Oxford's mayor, Richard Elliott, could not get help from the Highway Patrol. "They said they had no authority. That's when I called for the Army."

Frechette has his platoon dismount from the jeeps and fall into a straight line, riot-control formation, south of the square.

Meanwhile, I pull our lead Jeep up closer to the intersection and stay on the radio. Another squad of our MPs is deployed on foot car, crossing the intersection in the traditional riot-control wedge formation. I watch as they approach a lane. Then stop. Moments later the squad's sergeant, Geitz, a veteran of service in Korea, comes running back. Sergeant Geitz blurts out, "Sir, a group... Looks like Mississippi highway patrol" (stepping on his words as if two people were talking at once). "Maybe six or seven [quick breath]... They are just [quick breath] leaning against their patrol cars up that street." He looks back. "About twenty-five yards in front of my squad. Just staring at us... They are not moving. What do we do about them, lieutenant?" he shouts.

"Sergeant, move them out."

Geitz stares at me, eyes wide and disbelieving. His squad members, most in their late teens and early 20s, are about to clash face-to-face with other police, in uniforms as well. Our soldiers are everyone's next-door kids, not veteran police as most likely these state troopers are. Three days ago these draftees were directing traffic and handling drunks at Fort Dix. Now, suddenly, this morning, they're ordered to do this. It feels like I'm in a movie.

It's morning-quiet but for the bark of the sergeant's cadence count: "Hut ... Hut ... Hut." The wedge of soldiers moves up the lane toward the small cluster of patrolmen in their custom-fitted khaki uniforms.

One of the MPs stumbles on some curbing that he doesn't see because of his limited view behind the gas mask. Then Sergeant Geitz's bark comes out, strong and clear. "HEAR THIS, MOVE OUT! All personnel are to leave the area!"

Are we really doing this? Against our own?

111

Some of the highway troopers get into their cars in reaction to the sight of the MP squad—anonymous faces hidden behind gas masks—slowly closing on them. Rifles pointed upward, bayonets fixed. Others stand their ground, staring at the approaching soldiers. Two or three hold their arms out wide open. The gestures are clear, as if to say, "Hey, we're police too, just go around us."

From the jeep I can only stare. This is what our people are trained to do. I'm surprised that the squad members are doing so well. The first of Geitz's MPs to reach a patrolman lowers his rifle and prods him with his bayonet. No doubt now as to the army's intentions.

"You better not stick me with that thing, boy!" The MP sticks him.

He moves.

The other MPs quickly close in on each other as they're trained to do, while not breaking the discipline of the wedge. I watch as they use the butts of their rifles in order to move out the remaining patrolmen.

The Mississippian patrolmen curse as they move toward their squad cars, get in, and drive off. They circle back around us at the intersection. I know that that's not the peace sign I'm getting from one of Mississippi's best as he raises his middle finger from behind a passenger window.

This one scene tells me a lot. I now know why the highway patrol didn't meet us back at the Mississippi state line last night to escort us. And they're no longer playing a role anywhere on the campus here in Oxford, if they ever did last night.

So this is how it's going to be.

I react to what has just now happened across the street in the same way I did an earlier road incident, something between surprise and anger, with no time to think it over. Emotion comes before thought and reflection.

We still know very little of the bigger picture, only what we've just seen in front of our eyes, and this doesn't tell us much. We can place nothing into context and know of nothing else that might've been going on around us in the town over the last twelve hours. We're still in America, right?

At 0700 hours the next morning our security patrol of four jeeps, three men in each vehicle, moves out from our hillside encampment toward the campus and Baxter Hall, where Meredith is housed in a separate end unit of the dormitory building. A sergeant and Spec-4 Adams are in my jeep.

Our mission? The army doesn't deal in nuance. Simply put, just keep this guy, the lawyer, and the marshal alive.

James Meredith escorted to registration under MP guard.
(Photo by Ed Meek courtesy Department of Archives and Special Collections, University of Mississippi)

We pull up alongside the dormitory, and I go in to meet Mr. Meredith. Lieutenant Frechette is on the grounds with a small contingent of MPs. There was a bomb scare reported this morning at the dormitory that causes some understandable tension, along with the jeering students who have gathered on a corner across the street. One of them yells over, "Hey, where's the n----r?"

A few of Frechette's men are posted on the way up to the door and, as I go up the steps, I say, "AT EASE, men! I'll be in the area all day!"

It's a phrase normally used by senior officers who suddenly appear when enlisted men are engaged in a work detail or eating in the mess hall. The arriving officer understandably does not want them to interrupt whatever they're doing by having them snap to attention.

We second lieutenants use it among ourselves for its affected self-posturing humor, a humor that enlisted men often find amusing. Pete Frechette's people acknowledge my remark. I hope that it relaxes them a bit, particularly after what we've been through the last few days.

I should've ended my attempt at comic relief at this point. I go up to the door of Meredith's apartment unit. I think that only more of our battalion enlisted men are inside. I walk in. "AT EA...SE... EE," I begin and suddenly stop. I quickly realize that I'm in one of those uh-oh moments.

Deputy Attorney General Nicholas Katzenback and
Chief U.S. Marshal James McShane
*(Photo by Ed Meek courtesy Department of Archives and Special Collections,
University of Mississippi)*

No sooner do half the words come out than I find myself face-to-face with Mr. Katzenbach, Chief U.S. Marshal James P. McShane, General Billingslea, a bird colonel, my colonel, and assorted sergeants in the background. I catch Colonel Emmett Brice's eyes. Can't read them, but do read his mind and it's sending one of those "We need to talk, Lieutenant," signals. I'm too embarrassed to offer an apology or explanation and I move quickly toward an adjoining room. I walk in and hurriedly say "Hello, good morning" to three men, two of whom are whites in blue suits.

As was the case with an earlier meeting over at the Faculty House, it's been a while since I've been around civilians in suits. I speak the words so fast that it's almost impolite, for I'm focused on the third man in the room. I turn to the newly registered, twenty-nine-year-old student from Kosciusko, Mississippi.

"Mr. Meredith, I'm Lieutenant Gallagher of the 716th Military Police Battalion. I'm the officer in charge of the security patrol that will be with you when you are out on the campus."

"Pleased to meet you, Lieutenant," he says in a quiet voice that fits his slight stature.

It's followed by a soft handshake from him, not a grip. So this is the hand that has started it all. He looks so out of place, and I don't mean by the color of his skin. He's not in the campus fashion of the day, button-down collar, khakis, and penny loafers, but wears a suit neatly tailored to fit his thin, almost delicate, frame. His face is light brown with smooth skin. And he has no expression that one can interpret one way or another. I don't see any immediate picture of strength or purpose. All that will come to me later.

He gives a well-groomed impression that suggests a lot of thought has gone into his appearance this morning, including the highly polished shoes. I sense a kind of in-your-face, conscious choice not to go casual or try to look like the rest of the student body. As he is six or seven years older than his classmates anyway, his choice of dress is understandable, regardless of race. He can't blend in, so why even try?

In these first brief minutes I sense a quiet reserve about him. He does not appear to be a lead actor in the civil rights movement, a role that I find out later others will urge him to play. He does not want to be anybody's stalking horse or to be a part of anybody's movement. Whatever he accomplishes will be his individual success and his alone. And for his own purposes.

In this small room I try not to have my look at him turn into a stare, this person who is the cause behind the presence of twenty thousand U.S. Army soldiers, not to mention some elements of the Mississippi National Guard, in and around the town of Oxford today. So I turn and look around the room. While he and his room may be neat and orderly this morning, an adjoining room is not. My eye catches a table with half-filled Styrofoam coffee cups and an ashtray full of bent butts—signs, maybe, not of his long night,

115

but surely of the night that the other two men have just spent with him.

The moment becomes one of those awkward gatherings when strangers are thrown into close quarters by chance—as in a stalled office building elevator—and each one hopes superficial conversation will cover the wait. Whatever does one talk about at such a time? No one asks one of those "Where're you from, Lieutenant" questions. Maybe we should all just look down at our shoes as if we really are in an elevator. A moment later, a fourth suit comes into the room and says, "OK, let's go."

A simple "let's go." When we're so close to such an event, to such an incident, we never see it for what it is—out the door and into a little piece of history—but I find out later that that's what this morning will become. I stand back to be the last one out of the room. Protocol. I look at Meredith ahead of me. He stops for a second to look down at his shoes. Out of reflex I look down at mine. Army boots. Still a little mud.

Henry Gallagher is a retired lawyer living in Washington, D.C. with his wife, Le Chi, a retired librarian (and UT/Knoxville graduate). In September 1962, as a U.S. Army Military Police lieutenant, he served as the officer-in-charge (OIC) of a 12-man security team assigned to the student James Meredith. In 2023 the Minnesota History Theatre will be presenting a stage production of the story of the Southern Black student and Northern white lieutenant based in part on his book, *James Meredith and the Ole Miss Riot: A Soldier's Story* (University Press of Mississippi, 2012).

James Meredith attends his first class, Colonial American History.
The rest of the students left the room.
(Photo by Ed Meek courtesy Department of Archives and Special Collections,
University of Mississippi)

African Americans Recall Meredith's Impact

by Marquita Smith

Marquita Smith
(Photo courtesy of the author)

Sixty years ago, the nation looked on as James Meredith broke a major barrier becoming the first Black student to enroll at the University of Mississippi. His journey to the state flagship university represented resilience and resistance.

Despite Mississippi's denial of the federal court's mandate of Meredith's admission, his bravery and persistence inspired young people far and near. His quest for equality is etched in the memories of many.

Effie Burt was eight years old when James Meredith enrolled at the University. The longtime Oxford resident and international jazz singer said, "I remember more about having to go to Water Valley to get groceries instead of Oxford. I loved going to Oxford because my older sister and aunt lived there."

Burt's family lived on a farm between Oxford and Water Valley. "Aunt Sarah always kept lots of sweets, white bread and rolls. All at once, we were not getting any bread or sweets from them anymore. That's because my Uncle Elbert worked at the University of Mississippi in the cafeteria and the college was shut down," Burt explained.

Years later Effie Burt learned about Meredith's courage and what it meant for future students, faculty and staff, but she still

remembers the advice her parents shared with local families.

"My parents, Linder and Annie Lee Burt were community leaders. My dad was a masonic leader," she said. "They went into the community to tell the people not to go into Oxford, especially at night and told them to go to Water Valley or Batesville because it was bad people coming to Oxford to cause trouble."

Effie Burt
Photo by Kathleen W. Wickham

Still, "my father never let us feel that we were in danger. Burt said. "I do remember seeing my father praying a long time at night."

Her father wasn't the only one asking for God's protection for Meredith and others. In Ruleville, families also watched and prayed for Meredith.

Bobbi Allen, president of the Fannie Lou Hammer Memorial Garden and Museum Foundation, recalled her family gathered watching the news and listening to the radio to learn about the happenings in Oxford. "We feared for his life," Allen said. "People were afraid that he was going to be killed."

As a high school student, Allen said she and others understood the threat not just to Meredith, but to communities of color throughout the state as Mississippians protested Meredith's stand. Communities constantly prayed, she said.

"Mississippi was hot then, not just with heat," Allen said. "We had a lot of troubles here."

Professor Kenneth Sampson vividly remembers the day James Meredith enrolled at Ole Miss. "I had just finished graduate school," Sampson said, "and I had taken my first higher education job at what is now the University of Arkansas, Pine Bluff."

Meredith's journey was national news, and Sampson remembered watching television accounts of armed protesters rioting against thousands of U.S. Marshals, troops and the Mississippi National

Guard that President John F. Kennedy dispatched to protect Meredith on September 30, 1962.

Sampson, who retired after serving 51 years at Lane College in Jackson, Tennessee, said Blacks at that time thought the world would never change. Whether they were educators or local activists, people knew that integrating the University of Mississippi was a big deal, he said. Across the South, people had personal experiences of enduring segregation and racially motivated harassment. For Sampson it was beyond historical context and actual, lived, Jim Crow experiences.

The Civil Rights Movement, he said, was merely an extension of the protest that erupted in 1955 after the murder of Emmett Till, a 14-year-old who was accused of offending a white woman and tortured and lynched in Drew, Mississippi.

"Southern Blacks lived daily with intimidation and fear," Sampson said. "That's what made the timing and courage of James Meredith so exceptional. We were there in spirit with every step that the man took."

Retired CBS News Correspondent Randall Pinkston was in the sixth grade when Meredith enrolled at the University. He too recounted the mood of the nation, but more importantly

Mississippi. He recalled the firm public stance that Gov. Ross Barnett took to prohibit Meredith from attending classes at the University of Mississippi. In an attempt to block his admission, Barnett assumed the position of registrar.

Randall Pinkston
(Photo by Steven Laschever)

Pinkston was attending Smith Robinson Elementary, the first public school built for Blacks after the Civil War in Jackson, Mississippi, when Meredith was enrolled. The school, built in 1894 and closed in 1971, is now a museum and cultural center.

"We didn't see the images in real time. I remember seeing pictures of the riots and of Meredith walking across the campus during the same broadcast. The local news played both images on the same day."

Although still in elementary school, Pinkston said he was very much aware of what was happening in the northern part of the state.

"I started delivering the *Jackson Daily News*, when I was 12-years-old. It was the afternoon paper, and it was very pro-segregation and anti-civil rights. But I was reading the front page each day because I was folding and preparing to deliver the paper."

At that time, Jimmy Ward, was the editor of the *Jackson Daily News*. He wrote a daily front-page column, "Covering the Crossroads" that misrepresented the civil rights movement and expressed ardent segregationist views. He often expressed that "civil rights workers were outside agitators and communists. And, the colored people didn't need all of those demonstrations and protestors," Pinkston said. "Even at 11, I knew that wasn't the truth."

Even then, young Pinkston was delighted that Meredith had broken the color line at the University of Mississippi. But Pinkston said he never wanted to attend any white university in the state because he didn't want to go where he wasn't wanted.

Mississippi's racial history and tension was well documented and well known. In Kansas City, Carol A. Miller, M.D., anxiously watched television news documenting Meredith's campus experience. She said when she wanted more details and in-depth coverage about his encounters she turned to the major Black magazines Ebony and Jet. She watched and read closely. Her interest: Miller's paternal roots extend from an enslaved ancestor from a Winona plantation, three generations of Mississippians.

"There was so much vitriol around Meredith's enrollment," said Miller, a professor in the Department of Pediatrics at the University of California's San Francisco School of Medicine. "I didn't understand the major resistance to one young man trying to pursue an education. He wasn't asking to marry anyone's daughter or to be adopted by a white family. It was very discouraging for me.

I felt a lot of anger."

Miller, who was in high school at the time, expressed frustration with mixed messages. Black and white teachers, community and church leaders all said that education was the way to break down racial barriers, reduce poverty and combat systemic racism.

"There was so much hypocrisy. Didn't he deserve an education, especially at a public, state institution? Here he was trying to improve his level of competency and get a higher education."

Miller noted that whatever the level of educational attainment, Meredith persisted and endured. "He was a source of inspiration for me," she said.

While attending predominantly white institutions, Miller said she struggled financially and emotionally. People constantly questioned her intellectual capacity and created an exclusionary environment. Meredith modeled for her what it meant to succeed in the face of adversity, she said.

"What motivates someone to put themselves out there like that. I can't imagine the emotional abuse. His life was threatened," she said. "People had lost their lives for less. I was so fearful. Watching on television, you saw the leaders that should be protecting him too often engaged in the harassment."

While Miller and others expressed deep gratitude for the Meredith's contributions and the lasting impact he had on young African Americans, they also urged his protegés and the next generation to continue the quest for or equality and justice.

"Progress is still very necessary." Miller said. "Thank you for your bravery. Thank you for opening the door for me," she added. "His efforts had a ripple effect, and it really shaped thinking in terms of what I was entitled to as far as advancing my education."

Marquita Smith, Ed.D., is an associate professor and assistant dean for graduate programs in the School of Journalism & New Media at the University of Mississippi. A former Fulbright Scholar, she has lived and worked in Ghana and Liberia. As a Knight International Journalism Fellow, Smith created a judicial and justice reporting network in Liberia which continues to operate. She previously served as Division Chair for Communication and Fine Arts at John Brown University and is a former chair of the Association for Education in Journalism and Mass Communication's Commission on the Status of Minorities.

Mississippi in 1962

By William F. Winter

From, *Riot: Witness to Anger and Change,*
by Edwin E. Meek, Oxford, MS: Yoknapatawpha Press, 2015.
(reprinted with permission)

William Winter

From my home in Jackson in the early fall of 1962 I observed with increasing concern the state's hostile reaction to the decision of the U.S. Supreme Court ordering the admission of the first African-American student to my alma mater, the University of Mississippi. Founded in 1848, the school was an authentic product of the old South, and we, who are its alumni, take nostalgic pride in its Confederate heritage.

At the same time we recognize and applaud the growing academic reputation that it is achieving as a result of progressive academic leadership and the work of its many nationally acclaimed professors. In the autumn of 1962 we had further reason to be proud. The Ole Miss football team, winner of two recent national championships, was being picked by many sports writers to go undefeated. I could hardly wait for the season to begin. We had every reason to be hopeful and optimistic.

As an elected state official, I was acutely aware of the political pressure to resist the integration of the University. After all, almost a decade after the Brown decision declaring school segregation unconstitutional, there was not a single Black student enrolled in any public educational institution in Mississippi. I did not minimize the challenge of being the first. Yet I could not comprehend that Gov. Ross Barnett would blatantly refuse to obey an order of the U.S. Supreme Court, or that he would be so overwhelmingly supported in that position by so many normally reasonable and law-abiding citizens. I simply underestimated the fanatical level of resistance that had been built up over the years by the racist forces of the White Citizens Council and other white supremacy groups in the state.

Govenor Ross Barnet at football game
(Photo by Ed Meek courtesy Department of Archives and Special Collections, University of Mississippi)

The night before the campus riot, I became fully aware of the gravity of the situation. That evening, I was present at the football game in Jackson where the fuse of insurrection was lit. At halftime of the game with the University of Kentucky, Gov. Barnett strode to midfield and harangued an already passionate crowd by calling on every Mississippian to join him in resisting "the unlawful and tyrannical orders of the federal government," as he described the issue.

U.S. Marshals May Go To Campus Of Ole Miss

Gov. Barnett Needs Moral Support, Not Mob Violence, In This Crisis

(AN EDITORIAL)

Governor Ross Barnett has taken a firm stand and made a specific promise that the University of Mississippi will not be integrated next week. He rightly contends that public education is a state function in control of the state.

He has interposed himself between the federal government and any action it might try to take against Mississippians, especially those in official position.

What he needs from the average Mississippian in this crisis is strong moral support—not mob violence.

There is no greater service the people can render the governor and the state than to support him in this crusade to maintain the force and effect of States' Rights against federal encroachment.

Such support has come from every member of the Mississippi delegation in the Congress of the nation, except Rep. Frank Smith.

Such support should come from the grass-roots citizens of Mississippi. Mob violence in this situation would only make the governor's task more difficult.

Mississippians should permit our duly constituted authorities to handle the attempts at desegregation when and if they occur.

Step Is Considered By Dept. Of Justice

By BRANDT AYERS
Of The Clarion-Ledger Bureau

WASHINGTON—The U.S. Justice Department is considering the use of federal marshals to crack expected defiance of a court order to desegregate the University of Mississippi.

While the department would make no official statement, it was learned that the use of federal marshals was under consideration as a primary tool to pry open the University's doors to its first Negro student next week.

A department official, who declined to be quoted by name, Friday said, "The federal government has no alternative—we must enforce the orders of the court."

LIKELY STEPS

He admitted that the use of marshals would most likely be the first step if school officials obey Mississippi Gov. Ross Barnett's order to defy the court decree that it must admit James H. Meredith, a 29-year-old Negro Air Force veteran.

Meanwhile, a nearly unanimous pledge of "unqualified support" was sent to Gov. Barnett by the Mississippi congressional delegation.

In a telegram to the governor, Senators James O. Eastland and John Stennis and five of the six congressmen congratulated the governor on his stand.

Thursday night he called for the resignation of any state official not prepared to go to jail rather than bow to the court's order.

The 64-year-old governor told a state-wide radio and television audience, he would rather go to jail himself than submit to "the tyranny of judicial oppression."

Gov. Barnett's move was made in response to a ruling by United States Supreme Court Justice Hugo Black of Alabama which opened the way for Meredith to register at the University when the fall term begins Sept. 19.

Justice Black's order was backed up Friday from Meridian by Federal District Judge Sidney Mize, who previously had refused to issue such an order. He directed the university to admit Meredith and not to interfere.

NULLIFY SERIES

The order from Black and Mize nullified a series of orders by U.S. Circuit Court Judge Ben F. Cameron of Meridian which have delayed admission of the negro. All legal maneuvers now are apparently exhausted.

The only member of the Mississippi congressional delegation who refused to sign the telegram was Rep. Frank Smith, who was recently defeated by Rep. Jamie Whitten in a primary and has been named to the TVA Board by President Kennedy.

Reserve Action Nearing

Representatives Preparing To Act On Important Bill

WASHINGTON (AP)—A Democratic call for senators to close ranks behind President Kennedy's handling of the Cuban situation went out Friday as House leaders cleared the way for quick action on the President's Reserve mobilization bill.

Sen. Mike Mansfield of Montana the Senate Democratic leader, told his colleagues that Kennedy displayed "firmness and wisdom and responsibility" in his news

OFFICIALS IN HUDDLE TO PLAN ON STRATEGY

BY THE ASSOCIATED PRESS

State officials mapped strategy in secret Friday for an expected showdown over conflicting orders from Gov. Ross Barnett and U.S. Dist. Judge Sidney Mize in the University of Mississippi desegregation battle.

Mize, 74, a Gulfport jurist, handed down an order at Meridian directing the university to admit James Meredith, a Negro, next week. Mize said his order came on instructions from the U.S. 5th Circuit Court of Appeals at New Orleans.

His action was made public after Barnett directed state officials Thursday night to deny any desegregation order.

The state college board and university officials remained silent, although the board was in session. Barnett reportedly was in touch with the board.

Meredith, 29, an Air Force veteran from Kosciusko, was reported out of the state and not available for comment on the latest developments.

No Announcement By College Board

A U. S. Supreme Court order to admit Negro James Meredith responsible for operations and policies of the state institutions

(Clarion-Ledger, 9-15-62, Courtesy of Gannett Co., Inc.)

I attended the game with my wife Elise and two friends from Danville, Kentucky, who were our week-end guests. Our friends had seats in a different part of the stadium from ours. When we rejoined them after the game, we found them shaken and disbelieving. When the governor was introduced at halftime, virtually everyone in the stands stood up and cheered. Because our Kentucky friends chose not to stand, they were subjected to the vilest verbal abuse and threats. They could not understand what was happening. I could not comprehend it either, but it was a frightening experience. It brought back memories from the 1930s when as a schoolboy I had listened on our family radio to the ranting of Adolph Hitler. This political rally at our football game was like that, an ominous prelude to the following night's riot on the campus in Oxford. The football victory over Kentucky was totally overshadowed by the tragic events overwhelming our state.

Reports the day after the game noted extra traffic on the roads leading to Ole Miss. Apparently, it was not just that of students returning to campus. My family and I listened with increased foreboding to the disturbing news of a mob of hundreds of grim-looking men gathering at the University, intent on stopping James Meredith from entering and enrolling.

We watched President Kennedy's televised address asking for calm and no violence, but chaos soon prevailed. On the most shameful night that Ole Miss ever endured two men were killed; hundreds were wounded. A beautiful university lay battered and bleeding. As one of its proud graduates, I felt the deepest sense of outrage I have ever experienced.

Aftermath of the riot on the University of Mississippi campus.
(Photo by Ed Meek courtesy Department of Archives and Special Collections, University of Mississippi)

This ignominious scene that appeared like an open wound across the face of the state's oldest and most prestigious public institution of higher learning could well have resulted in its demise. Certain fanatics and some political leaders wanted it closed rather than accept a Black student.

After the initial shock and anger over the tragic event had begun to subside, many of us came to recognize it was not just the violent rioters who bore responsibility for the tragedy. All of us—state and university officials, proud alumni, confused students, indifferent citizens—had acquiesced in one way or another in creating a "closed society" that brought us to the infamy of that shameful day. The guilt was on the hands of us all.

That event was over fifty years ago, and I still suffer from the anguish of those tragic days. To recount it now is to test my acceptance that it could ever have happened.

As early as the morning after the riot, even before anyone could assess the extent of the carnage, I was heartened to hear on a local television station a leading Jackson businessman, William H. Mounger, the president of the company which owned that station, deliver an impassioned address to his fellow Mississippians denouncing the violence and calling for an end to resisting the Court's order.

Other similar statements soon followed from church, business and civic leaders from across the state. For the first time since the Brown decision, nine years before, it appeared that public sentiment was moving in a sensible direction. However, once more I failed to gauge the extent of the continuing force of the Citizens Council.

To my alarm I began to detect the development of a shrewdly orchestrated public relations plan that sought to whitewash the state's role in the fiasco and to put the entire blame on President Kennedy and his brother, Robert, the attorney general. They were made out to be the villains. They became the enemy. At the same time, the federal court was having to deal with the contempt charges it had levied on Gov. Barnett and the Board of Trustees of the Institutions of Higher Learning. A contingent of federal troops and U. S. Marshals was forced to remain on the campus to ensure there would be no more trouble.

About the only bright spot was the unblemished record of the University football team. There were few other heroes. Some of our best professors began to look for a less turbulent academic scene. Many students did not return for the second semester. There is no accurate way to predict how many prospective students did not show up the following fall, but enrollment was down.

The school and the state of Mississippi had paid a frightful price for the horrendous experience. But the struggle had not ended. It would be another decade before things returned to normal.

Politician at Neshoba County Fair
(Photo by Ed Meek courtesy Department of Archives and Special Collections, University of Mississippi)

The first year immediately after the riot, we had to listen to some of the most racially inflammatory political campaign rhetoric I had ever heard, especially in races for governor, attorney general and superintendent of education. Violence continued in many communities over voting rights. In June of that year Medgar Evers, state field director for the NAACP, was assassinated at his home in Jackson. The succeeding year saw the murder of three young civil rights workers in Neshoba County and the burning and bombing of over 50 Black churches across the state.

A direct result of the riot, the continuing violence and the resistance to integration was the passage in the summer of 1964 of the Civil Rights Act, outlawing segregation in all public places. I had been elected state treasurer in the summer of 1963. One of my most important duties was to oversee the issuance and sale of state bonds. On a trip to New York City in 1964 to promote the sale of a school issue, I was shocked to discover that even though our state had an acceptable credit rating, we were paying significantly higher interest on similarly rated bonds than most other states. One issue floated on Wall Street in 1965 had no bidders at all because of the stigma resulting from the 1962 riot and the subsequent violence arising out of the state's civil rights resistance.

The next major action at the federal level occurred with the passage of the 1965 Voting Right Act. That really changed the political system: for the first time African Americans had access to the power of the vote. Whereas the Act did not solve all of the problems, it changed the political landscape of this state forever and pointed the way to what would hopefully be the entry of our state into the national mainstream.

I was a candidate for governor in 1967. Running in a field that included Ross Barnett and the Citizen Council's candidate, John Bell Williams, I led in the first primary. But I was overwhelmed in the runoff for my perceived "moderate" stand on the integration issue. I was denounced by my opponents as being supportive of the Kennedys in the admission of Meredith to Ole Miss.

However, the once impenetrable wall of massive resistance was beginning to crack under the impact of the Civil Rights and Voting Rights Acts. A growing public acceptance of change was taking place. By 1970 the statehouses of most Southern states, including Mississippi, were being occupied by a series of progressive governors, both Democrat and Republican. Blatant appeals based on racial prejudice were no longer effective. Hundreds of Black local officials were beginning to be elected across the South. Robert Clark became Mississippi's first Black legislator since reconstruction.

In the ensuing decade of the 1970s all of the formerly all-white state institutions of higher learning were recruiting and enrolling increasing numbers of Black students, who soon advanced into leadership roles. Since then, four Black student body presidents have been elected at Ole Miss. Seventeen percent of the students now are African Americans.

As these laudable developments and the racial battles of the 1960's become a distant memory, we now have reason to celebrate our release from the fears and inhibitions of the past. We owe that progress to so many brave men and women.

I once remarked to my dear friend, Myrlie Evers, the widow of the martyred civil rights leader, Medgar Evers, that we white folks owed as much to him and James Meredith and their brave comrades as Black folks do. They freed us, too. All of us, Black and white alike, had been victims of a cruel system of apartheid that kept us all enslaved.

I have always believed that Mississippi has much to teach the rest of the country about race relations. Having been the state where extreme battles over integration were fought, we can now appreciate more fully the progress we have made.

The harsh lessons, which we learned in the racial confrontations of the 1960s, must not be forgotten in these more recent years. Having now preserved the prestige and respect of Ole Miss and all of the rest of our state's cherished educational institutions, all of which were threatened by the irresponsible and mindless forces of fear and intolerance a half-century ago, we must now see to it that future generations do not ever again succumb to demagogic appeals to prejudice and bigotry. They held us back for too long.

Until James Meredith came along we were prisoners of a system that held us all down, that dictated what we felt free to say, whom we could associate with, and how we lived our lives. We were all in bondage to an indefensible way of life that was at odds with the ideals on which this country was founded. This state, Mississippi, has now begun to come into its own as a result of that liberation.

William F. Winter (1923-2020) served as Governor of Mississippi from 1980 to 1984. Previously he was elected to the offices of state representative, state tax collector, state treasurer and lieutenant governor. He was chairman of the Southern Regional Education Board, the Appalachian Regional Commission, the Southern Growth Policies Board, the Commission on the Future of the South, the National Civic League, the Kettering Foundation, the Mississippi Department of Archives and History. He was a member of President Clinton's National Advisory Board on Race and was instrumental in the founding of the William Winter Institute for Racial Reconciliation at the University of Mississippi. He was awarded the Profile in Courage Award by the John F. Kennedy Library Foundation and is the author of *The Measure of Our Days.*

Graduation Day

By James Meredith

From *Three Years in Mississippi*. Bloomington, IN: Indiana
University Press, 1966
(Reprinted with permission)

James Meredith
(Photo by Kathleen W. Wickham)

Perhaps the most remarkable achievement of my three years
in Mississippi fighting the system of "White Supremacy" is that I
survived. Mississippi is well known for many things, but it is best
known for eliminating those who threaten the continued existence
of "White Supremacy."

The use of raw, demonstrative violence has become a religion to
the whites. Its ceremonial and ritualistic aspects are a vital part of
the Mississippi way of life. The very existence of the white society
requires periodic doses of this violent religious lunacy; for without
sacrificial violence to bind it together, the white world would fall
apart.

Knowing this, my Air Force squadron commander, a white
Mississippian of the aristocratic class, assured me in 1955 that
Mississippi whites were prepared to kill all the Negroes and half
the whites in order to preserve "White Supremacy." Mississippi and
Mississippians had not changed.

My goal in Mississippi was to break the system of "White
Supremacy" at any cost. I felt a "Divine responsibility" to accomplish
this mission. The crucial question was how to work towards this

end. At a very early age I established the three theoretical interim goals to be achieved along the way. I stress "theoretical" because to me each of these goals was a separate step or focal point. I never considered the accomplishment of any one of them as being necessary to attain my ultimate purpose. The three goals were to become "unadjectived" or not limited to a single definition; to run for governor of Mississippi with 100 percent of the Negro vote; and to get a degree from the University of Mississippi. These were to be accomplished in reverse order.

After three years what did the record show? I had earned a degree from the University of Mississippi and had seriously disrupted and undermined the system of white supremacy. Although my receiving a degree from the university had not broken the system, I had surely disrupted it.

As to running for governor I concluded it would be folly to bid for the Negro vote. There were over a half-million Negroes of voting age in Mississippi, yet less than six percent were allowed to vote. The question of becoming a man was even further removed. There is no doubt that at the end of my three years in Mississippi more stress had been placed on my being a Negro than ever before in my life. The aim of reaching a stage where a Negro is judged simply by the standards of humanity without regard to race was indeed still a long way in the future.

Many of my friends and relatives had been looking forward to my graduation day. Mrs. Kenny Smith, the wife of Robert L.T. Smith, Jr., had vowed many times that she was going to "that graduation if it is the last thing in the world that I ever do." I didn't really think that she would go, because she seldom went anywhere except to work and to church, but she stuck by her pledge and came. There were so many Negroes going that we formed an unplanned caravan which, of course, included the U.S. marshals, whose force was increased by three or four times its regular size.

Following two cars of marshals, I led the caravan in my wife's well-publicized Thunderbird. My wife and son and the Smiths were riding with me. We drove to Kosciusko where we stopped at my parents' home and ate the dinner which my mother had proudly prepared. The caravan was joined here by several cars of relatives and home-town friends. Some of them had come from thousands of miles away to attend my graduation.

In addition to the general excitement of the two-hundred-mile trip, the atmosphere was filled with the consciousness of possible trouble. From Kosciusko, we drove north on the Natchez Trace Parkway, a federal government project, where the facilities are not officially segregated. Just before we turned off the parkway onto a Mississippi highway, we stopped at a gas station to use the rest rooms because they were not segregated.

Shortly after we turned off the parkway, the Mississippi state troopers, who were covering the caravan in large numbers, began maneuvering in and out of the line of cars. The marshals tightened the caravan ranks and increased the speed. One of the troopers suddenly sped along past the caravan and tried to maneuver his car in between mine and the marshals' car. By closing up behind him, a marshal, along with the one immediately ahead of me, managed to prevent the trooper from getting in front of me. He then raced off ahead of us and parked in an intersection. They didn't bother us any more after that.

The March to the Grove. The student captain of my group was the newly elected vice president of the student body. He had won the election on an anti-Meredith campaign. He was also a political science major and we had had classes together each term. I don't know if he ever spoke to me, although he was a very articulate individual. But he just didn't recognize my existence or that such things as Negroes could have human or equal rights. He had the responsibility of seeing that everyone was in his proper place in the line. He didn't call my name very many times, and when he did, he did it categorically.

Surprisingly, there was no opposition to being my marching mate. My marching partner in the first line-up was a young lady, and I heard some of the other graduates asking her how she was so lucky to get all of that "free publicity," assuming that she would be in the papers and on television with me. She appeared disappointed when a student came in late and the line-up had to be changed. No unpleasant remarks were made by the students, so that I could hear them.

On our march to the Grove we passed through the Lyceum Building where the U.S. government had set up its headquarters on September 30, 1962, the day I came to the campus. As I passed, I took special notice of the bullet holes that were still there, a consequence of the fighting between the state of Mississippi and the federal government of the United States. I had looked at these bullet holes many times.

We marched on past the statue of the Confederate soldier, the symbol of the blood that had been shed one hundred years ago in defense of the system of "White Supremacy." It was at the foot of this statue that General Edwin A. Walker had spoken to the crowd on the night of the revolt of the state of Mississippi.

We ended our march in the Grove, where the graduation exercises were being held in the open air. This was near the Circle where most of the riot had taken place on September 30. To one who knows the realities of life in Mississippi, the most striking thing about the Grove was the Negroes scattered throughout the audience. They were there in large numbers. Frankly, I was very surprised to see so many Negroes, but very pleased indeed.

James Meredith receives diploma from Chancellor Williams.
(Photo courtesy of Bill Miles)

The Ceremony. After taking my place among the graduates, I looked out at the curious and staring audience. Cameras were clicking in every direction. There in the audience was my seventy-two-year-old father with my three-year-old son. Throughout his life he had given his all in an effort to make Mississippi and the world free for his children and his children's children. He had lived to see the day that he had always longed for but had never really expected to see. Sitting on his knee was my son, not yet aware of the existence of the system of "White Supremacy" that would seek in every possible way to render him less than human. He seemed quite amused by the events. My gratification came from the hope that my son might be a future Governor or President.

James Meredith at his 1963 graduation ceremony.
Photo by Bill Miles, courtesy of the Department of Archives and Special Collections, University of Mississippi

The ceremony was routine. The speeches were rather mild, only one speaker referred to the controversial issues. He mentioned something about the encroachment upon Mississippi's prerogatives by the federal government. When my name was called the Chancellor handed me my diploma, shook my hand, and offered his congratulations.

I noticed two familiar faces. One was my old Negro friend on the campus, who had touched me with his broom and showed support under pressure. At the ceremony he kept his distance, however, standing about fifty yards away at the corner of a building. After all, he had to live there after I was gone. The other person was James

Allen Jr., the only Black face among the marshals, news reporters, and cameramen near the stage. His boldness had placed him in a position to get the closest of all photographs of the Chancellor handing me my diploma.

After the ceremony, we marched briefly back to the campus to discard our caps and gowns. Just as I stepped outside the building two young boys rushed up to me; one of them grabbed my hand, gave it a hard squeeze and said, "I just wanted to congratulate you!" The two boys identified themselves as the grandsons of an English teacher at the University of Mississippi.

I had passed the word to many of the Negroes to come and Baxter Hall where I had spent my nights at the university. The marshals packed their shotguns and tear gas and made ready to leave the campus, hopefully for the last time. They were ready to end their mission in Mississippi. We had seen a lot of days together.

I had agreed to leave Mississippi temporarily after graduation. Many people felt that it was for the best to allow a resettling, or transition, period. I always seemed to be either coming in or out of Mississippi while I was at the university. On August 18, 1963, I left again with U.S. marshals headed to Tennessee. A serious question occurred to me: Did this constitute the privilege of attending the school of my choice?

We drove at top speed down the four-lane highway that led to Memphis. But this still was not fast enough for my friend and great freedom fighter, Robert L.T. Smith, Jr., who rode with me. Everyone was silent. Finally, looking at the marshals' cars in front and in back of us, Robert said, "J, was it like this all of the time?" Without waiting for a reply, he continued, "Man, I don't see how you stood it! I just don't see how you could take it!"

At last we arrived at my cousin Katherine's house in Memphis. She and her husband had attended the graduation exercises and were waiting for us when we arrived. In September of 1962 it was at Katherine's house that the deputy marshals had begun their watch over me, and it was fitting that they should say goodbye at the same spot. These men dedicated to the idea of human equality and freedom for all were as good an example of the American ideal as could possibly be found.

James Meredith and his parents Moses and Roxie Meredith
(Photo by Wofford Smith, courtesy of Robert Smith)

My father and mother had come to Memphis to bid me farewell. After a while my father took me aside to express his satisfaction at having lived to see this day. He had watched the whites at the graduation ceremony. He knew these people. For seventy-two years he had seen the "meanness" and contempt in their looks. Now he had witnessed a fading of the all-pervading hatred which accompanied every contact between the whites and Blacks in Mississippi. At least for one day it had been missing from their faces. Considering my University of Mississippi ordeal his conclusion about the Mississippi whites surprised me.

"These people can be decent," he said.

My exit from Mississippi on August 18, 1963, marked the end of a three-year struggle to break the system of white supremacy and to carry out what I felt was a divine responsibility.

It was the end of a long day.

James Meredith and son Dr. Joseph Meredith at the
James Meredith statue commemoration Oct. 1, 2006, at the
University of Mississippi.
*(Photo by Robert Jordan, courtesy of University Marketing and Communications,
University of Mississippi)*

Bibliography

Doyle, William, *An American Insurrection: James Meredith and the Battle of Oxford, Mississippi, 1962* (Anchor Books/Random House, 2001).

Gallagher, Henry, *James Meredith and the Ole Miss Riot: A Soldier's Story* (University Press of Mississippi, 2012).

Gilliam, Dorothy, *Trailblazer: A Pioneering Journalist's Fight to Make the Media Look More Like America* (Center Point Books/Hachette, 2019).

Meredith, James, *Three Years in Mississippi*, (Bloomington, IN: Indiana University Press, 1966).

Wickham, Kathleen, *We Believed We Were Immortal: Twelve Reporters Who Covered the 1962 Integration Crisis at Ole Miss* (Yoknapatawpha Press, 2017).

Wilkie, Curtis, *Dixie: A Personal Odyssey Through Events That Shaped the Modern South* (Lisa Drew Books/Scribner, 2001).

Winter, William F., *Afterword, Riot: Witness to Anger and Change*, by Edwin E. Meek (Yoknapatawpha Press, 2015).

Acknowledgments

Creating *James Meredith: Breaking the Barrier* took the goodwill and support of a variety of people and organizations, starting with James Meredith himself, who told me he supported the project thus opening the door for recruiting writers, publishers and photographers to sign on, without pay, for their contributions.

Dr. Shawnboda Mead, vice-chancellor for diversity and engagement at the University of Mississippi, deserves special recognition for her support and encouragement for this project. I also wish to acknowledge her expert leadership of the university's James Meredith 60th anniversary committee. *Breaking the Barrier* is designed as a commemorative book for the 2022 activities honoring Meredith, serving as a capsule summary of the events leading to his admission to the University of Mississippi as the first African-American to be admitted to any public school in Mississippi. Dr. Mead supported the book from my proposal through publication. Her support is much appreciated.

Appreciation is expressed to the following authors and publishers for allowing re-publication of portions of the following:

Doyle, William, *An American Insurrection: James Meredith and the Battle of Oxford, Mississippi, 1962* (Anchor Books/Random House, 2001).

Gallagher, Henry, *James Meredith and the Ole Miss Riot: A Soldier's Story* (University Press of Mississippi, 2012).

Gilliam, Dorothy, *Trailblazer: A Pioneering Journalist's Fight to Make the Media Look More Like America* (Center Point Books/Hachette, 2019).

Meredith, James, *Three Years in Mississippi*, (Bloomington, IN: Indiana University Press, 1966).

Wickham, Kathleen, *We Believed We Were Immortal: Twelve Reporters Who Covered the 1962 Integration Crisis at Ole Miss* (Yoknapatawpha Press, 2017).

Wilkie, Curtis, *Dixie: A Personal Odyssey Through Events That Shaped the Modern South* (Lisa Drew Books/Scribner, 2001).

Winter, William F., *Afterword, Riot: Witness to Anger and Change,* by Edwin E. Meek (Yoknapatawpha Press, 2015).

Please note: Because these are excerpts for a commemorative book notes and source lists are not included. Readers interested in supporting information should consult the original publications.

Three contributors, Jesse Holland, Sidna Brower Mitchell, Marquita Smith, are also thanked for their original contributions. They produced outstanding work on a short time-schedule, meeting their deadlines with grace and enthusiasm.

Appreciation is also expressed to the photographers whose work appears here: Dan Brennan, Kea Duree, Henry Gallagher, Marie Gerard, Alain Guihard, Steven Laschever, Bill Miles, Enrique Shore, Doug Sanford, Wofford Smith, Robert Smith and Curtis Wilkie. Their images uniquely supported the narrative.

I am also forever grateful to the staff of the Department of Archives and Special Collections at the University of Mississippi for granting permission to reprint so many photographs. Their inclusion of the events from 1962 support the dramatic tales told by the authors.

Larry Wells, the director of Yoknapatawpha Press, did not hesitate when I approached him with this project. His deft editing and commitment kept the project on track to meet our deadline. Mon ami.

CPSIA information can be obtained
at www.ICGtesting.com
Printed in the USA
LVHW042249220922
729060LV00003B/567